OBAMANOMICS

OBAMANOMICS
HOW BOTTOM-UP ECONOMIC PROSPERITY WILL REPLACE TRICKLE-DOWN ECONOMICS

John R. Talbott

Seven Stories Press

NEW YORK • TORONTO • LONDON • MELBOURNE

A Seven Stories Press First Edition

Seven Stories Press
140 Watts Street
New York, NY 10013
www.sevenstories.com

In Canada: Publishers Group Canada, 559 College Street, Suite 402, Toronto, ON M6G 1A9

In the UK: Turnaround Publisher Services Ltd., Unit 3, Olympia Trading Estate, Coburg Road, Wood Green, London N22 6TZ

In Australia: Palgrave Macmillan, 15–19 Claremont Street, South Yarra, VIC 3141

College professors may order examination copies of Seven Stories Press titles for a free six-month trial period. To order, visit www.sevenstories.com/textbook or send a fax on school letterhead to (212) 226-1411.

Book design by Jon Gilbert

Library of Congress Cataloging-in-Publication Data

Talbott, John R., 1955-
 Obamanomics : how bottom-up prosperity will replace trickle-down economics / John R. Talbott.
   p. cm.
 ISBN 978-1-58322-865-4 (pbk.)
 1. United States--Economic conditions--21st century. 2. Economic forecasting--United States. I. Title.
 HC106.83.T35 2008
 330.973--dc22

                              2008022402
Printed in the USA.

9 8 7 6 5 4 3 2 1

If we lived in a State where virtue was profitable, common sense would make us good, and greed would make us saintly. And we'd live like animals or angels in the happy land that needs no heroes. But since in fact we see that avarice, anger, envy, pride, sloth, lust and stupidity commonly profit far beyond humility, chastity, fortitude, justice and thought, and have to choose, to be human at all . . . why then perhaps we must stand fast a little—even at the risk of being heroes.

Sir Thomas More, *A Man for All Seasons*

Few will have the greatness to bend history itself; but each of us can work to change a small portion of events, and in the total of all those acts will be written the history of this generation. . . . It is from numberless diverse acts of courage and belief that human history is thus shaped. Each time a man stands up for an ideal, or acts to improve the lot of others, or strikes out against injustice, he sends forth a tiny ripple of hope, and crossing each other from a million different centers of energy and daring, those ripples build a current which can sweep down the mightiest walls of oppression and resistance.

Robert F. Kennedy

CONTENTS

PREFACE

In writing this book, I was guided by a philosophy practiced by Barack Obama, namely, it does little good to try to assign blame for our current problems, as this only causes argument and dissension among us. We all know where we are, and it isn't enough to know how we got here. What we want now are solutions.

We are a peaceful nation at war. We are a caring nation whose citizens are hurting from home foreclosures and unaffordable healthcare. We are a proud nation held in contempt by countries the world over. We are a fiscally responsible people whose government is $10 trillion in debt and facing a very serious housing and financial crisis. We are a nation of laws that are being written by corporate special interests. And we are a country, founded on equality, liberty, justice and opportunity for all, that is slowly devolving into an unjust class society where life success is based more on inherited position and connections than individual effort and merit.

Even though times seem bleak, our problems can be conquered. I am confident of this, because I believe almost all of our problems are a result of a few fundamental errors our country has made that can be corrected. If we correct these fundamental mistakes, solutions to our bigger problems will become more evident and the practical means to implement them will become clear.

Obama has been criticized during the election campaign for spending too much time talking about big general principles and not getting into the specifics of his proposals. First of all, this is not entirely true. Secondly, he may be on to something. I think he understands that our problems are not solvable unless we address these fundamental issues. Our country was built on fundamental principles, and we have slowly moved away from them.

I don't want to try to convince you here of Barack's trustworthiness or motives. That is something each of you will have to decide on your own. Throughout the book, I present Obama's positions on issues and problems facing the country, and speak in some detail about his policy prescriptions. But I did not want this book to be solely about policy. I wanted to dig deeper, to examine Obama's core beliefs and better understand his underlying logic and strategy. At times I have disagreed with his approach, and when I do, I say so. I have also attempted to give the reader a better understanding of the underlying problems Obama will face. Using my background in finance, I try to give the reader a firm grasp of the magnitude and scope of these problems. And finally, I give my thoughts on the additional steps Obama might take, once in office, to succeed in overcoming the many challenges ahead.

I could not have attempted to write this book without the considerable help of others. I am indebted to my cousin, Alex Talbott, who listened to me for months on end and helped me improve my argument. My good friend George Marshall reminded me constantly the emphasis of this book was not the stock market or hedge funds or private equity firms; it was always our citizens' well-being. My publisher, Dan Simon at Seven Stories Press, is to be commended for taking a chance on a text that bigger corporate-owned publishers would have dismissed as heresy, since it argues that corporate special interests in Washington were the root cause of almost all of our problems. He has been extremely helpful in editing this text, and he contributed greatly to its overall readability and the coherence of its arguments. He has been a pleasure to work with. I also would like to thank Ruth Weiner, Crystal Yakacki, Theresa Noll, and the rest

of the gang at Seven Stories Press for their excellent work on my
behalf.

I hope you sit back and enjoy the book in the spirit in which it was
written: to help all Americans find a way to take back control of
our government, to begin to address problems affecting us, and to
gain a better understanding of this skinny kid with the funny
sounding name who just might be the leader we have been looking
for.

John R. Talbott
johntalbs@hotmail.com

INTRODUCTION

> *It was the best of times, it was the worst of times, it*
> *was the age of wisdom, it was the age of foolishness,*
> *it was the epoch of belief, it was the epoch of*
> *incredulity, it was the season of Light, it was the sea-*
> *son of Darkness, it was the spring of hope, it was the*
> *winter of despair, we had everything before us, we*
> *had nothing before us . . .*
> —Charles Dickens, *A Tale of Two Cities*[1]

So begins Dickens's epic tale of life in London and Paris in 1775, prior to the beginning of the French Revolution. America today faces a similar dichotomy between foolishness and wisdom. Much of the focus in the media has been on the great disparity in wealth and income between our richest and poorest citizens, but the problems facing America run much deeper than simple economic inequality.

Yes, we do live in a society in which our chief executives earn 465 times as much per year as their workers.[2] Our wealthiest Americans live in 20,000+ square foot homes, while millions of Americans are risking losing their homes to foreclosure. The rich buy boats and cars and diamonds and jewels and throw lavish parties, while their fellow citizens scrape by trying to pay the rent and feed their families. The top 1 percent of Americans controls nearly 40 percent of the country's wealth.[3] One hundred and thirteen million Americans suffer from chronic illnesses such as heart disease and diabetes, 47 million have no health insurance, and 37 million live in poverty that leaves them unable to properly care for their children.[4]

Sometimes these separate worlds collide. At the Kentucky Derby on the first Saturday in May each year, corporate executives and celebrities sip mint juleps on Millionaires Row, they pay as much as $1 million to watch a two minute horse race. In the horse stables on the back stretch at Churchill Downs, just a quarter mile away, young immigrant hot walkers and grooms earn a couple of dollars an hour off the books, and often end up sleeping in the stables on the straw next to the horses. The horses they care for are valued in the tens of millions of dollars by a society that puts almost no value on these young people's lives and their dreams.

In addition to vast inequality in our country, there are many examples of gross injustice across this great land. We have spent close to $1 trillion to fight terrorism worldwide, and yet the number of terrorists in the world has increased many fold, and Osama Bin Laden remains at large. The majority of our defense budget goes to very large for-profit defense contractors to build advanced weapons systems, while our troops risk their lives on the battlefield for meager salaries. Tens of thousands of veterans returning home find inadequate health care, poor job prospects and end up having to use food stamps to feed their families. Halliburton, thanks to no-bid contracts it has been given in Iraq and in New Orleans after hurricane Katrina, has seen its stock price increase more than 700 percent, while 4,000 body bags have returned from Iraq, and citizens of New Orleans had to sit on the roofs of their flooded houses for days waiting to be rescued.

In a world that is slowly exhausting its supply of traditional energy sources and faces the threat of global warming, the average American consumes twenty-two times as much energy as the citizens in a typical developing country,[5] produces eighteen times as much waste,[6] and twenty to forty times as much carbon dioxide per capita.[7]

We have a government that is $10 trillion in debt and faces an additional $50 trillion liability in order to fund its retirement and health care systems.[8] If nothing is done about these debts today, it is projected that our children will face tax rates double to triple what we have paid in order to fund our extravagances and repay our debts.[9]

Our public schools are in disarray, with one third of high school seniors unable to do the simple mathematics required for productive employment[10] and 60 percent of young people age eighteen to twenty-four unable to locate Iraq on a map.[11] Higher-income Americans send their children to private elementary and high schools at costs that can range from $10,000 to $30,000 per year per child. The best determinant of outstanding educational performance is not the quality of our teachers or of our schools, but the incomes of the students' parents. Being born into the right family in the right neighborhood in America is more important in predicting future career success than anything else.

Homeowners face possible housing price declines of 20 to 40 percent across America, and as many as ten million Americans may lose their homes to foreclosure, while our government officials do little but bail out their investment banking and hedge fund cronies who have given millions to their political campaigns.[12] We face a financial crisis in this country caused by excessive borrowing, debt leverage, and fraud in the banking and mortgage system that went largely unregulated by a government corrupted by Wall Street and corporate money and lobbying.

We have opened our country to the global marketplace, but not before assuring our largest corporations that their contracts will be honored, their manufacturing plants protected, and their intellectual property rights and patents secured. No similar safeguards were created to protect our workers from the onslaught of having to compete with billions of underemployed workers around the world, or to protect our consumers from unsafe toys, pharmaceuticals and other products from abroad, or to protect the global environment from massive increases in global pollution.

All is not well in America. Our government has an annual operating deficit of close to $400 billion, and this number would be closer to $2 trillion if the shortfalls in Social Security and Medicare were amortized and included.[13] Our current account trading deficit with our international trading partners is close to $700 billion per year. Real wages for our workers have not increased materially in thirty years. Home prices are collapsing, our financial system and our banks are in peril, and our stock market is down approximately 15 to 20 percent from its peak, and dropping.[14] Actual unemployment, including all those of working age that are not fully employed, is more than 15 percent of our workforce.[15] Our healthcare system is a mess, and our public schools are not much better. Our state and municipal governments face funding shortfalls as property tax appraisals decline and many of their workers begin to retire. And the greatest number of our most productive workers, our beloved baby boomers, are just now beginning to retire and slow their voracious consumption that has driven our economy for decades.

Into this morass strides a "skinny kid with a funny name," Barack Obama, someone who, by his own admission, probably shouldn't be here. As he likes to describe it,

> . . . my presence on this stage is pretty unlikely. My father was a foreign student, born and raised in a small village in Kenya. He grew up herding goats, went to school in a tin-roof shack. His father—my grandfather—was a cook, a domestic servant to the British. . . . [My mother] was born in a town on the other side of the world, in Kansas. Her father worked on oilrigs and farms through most of the Depression. My parents shared not only an improbable love, they shared an abiding faith in the possibilities of this nation. They would give me an African name, Barack, or "blessed," believing that in a tolerant America your name is no barrier to success. They imagined—they imagined me going to the best schools in the land, even though they weren't rich, because in a generous America you don't have to be rich to achieve your potential.[16]

There is no question that Obama is a unique and gifted person. His oratory is renowned, and his presidential campaign was filled with inspirational talks to tens of thousands of supporters. A Pew Research Center poll conducted in March of 2008 asked respondents about the positive and negative qualities they associated with the candidates. Eighty percent found Obama inspiring and 78 percent found him honest, patriotic and down-to-earth, while only 16 percent found him phony and a measly 13 percent said he was hard to like.[17] In every category, Obama dominated Hillary Clinton, his major rival for the Democratic presidential nomination. In addition, a majority of respondents said that Obama made them feel hopeful and proud about themselves.

What do these admirable personal qualities have to do with solving our nation's most pressing problems? Everything. This book hopes to demonstrate that what is lacking in America is a leader who is honest and who can inspire our citizens to take their government back from the special interests, with their corrupting influence, and re-instill in it the principles of justice and fairness this country was founded on. These problems cannot be addressed until they are spoken of honestly, until our government and its officials begin to emphasize justice. And they cannot be solved by individuals competing with one another. They can only be solved through cooperation. Obama's goal is to stimulate that kind of cooperation among all Americans.

John McCain, the Republican nominee for president, is a seventy-two year old white Republican male married to the heiress of a beer distribution fortune who sees little need to change the course we are on. He supported a continuation of the war in Iraq, and even suggested we might be there for a hundred more years. He favored keeping the healthcare system just like it is, not mentioning that he himself would not qualify for most health insurance plans today given his prior condition of having had skin cancer. He suggested that the best plan to address the financial crisis on Wall Street was to do nothing unless the entire economic system were at risk. Similarly, he did not want to see the government get in the business of bailing out homeowners who found their homes to be worth less than their mortgages. Although initially calling the Bush tax cuts for the rich unjust and indefensible, he reversed himself in the campaign and came out for extending them for the wealthiest Americans. He is a military man whose father and grandfather were admirals in the navy; he sees conflict as a natural means of settling disputes, and would not shy away from utilizing all means at our disposal to fight terrorism and our enemies.

Bush's ineptitude in fighting the war, managing the economy, regulating Wall Street, and responding to Katrina, as well as his sellout of the government to big business, have ironically reinforced his view that government cannot be trusted to do the people's business. By performing his job so poorly, Bush has laid the groundwork for arguing that government is ineffective.

Obama's message during his presidential campaign was one of hope and change. While constantly drawn into detailed policy debates by the competition, Obama's strength was in addressing much deeper philosophical issues in the campaign. He often utilized his knowledge of the Constitution to query audiences on how our founding fathers might approach a particular problem we face today. Emphasizing personal liberty, equality, and economic justice, Obama was able to describe a country in which economic opportunity would be available to all under an Obama administration.

He explained that a healthy economy is a bottom-up economy, not a top-down economy dependent on trickle-down economics. In a bottom-up economy, the rules of business and government are fair and apply to all. There is a level playing field. In such an environment, people's enthusiasm and motivations are maximized. They feel that their personal success will be determined by their hard work and effort, not by who they know or who they are related to. Obama believes that the key to a growing and prosperous economy is a motivated workforce that is engaged and constantly thinking about how it can improve itself, its company's products and services, and its country. In a rigged system in which big business controls our government, such motivation is impossible. Obama believes that all will benefit from the system he envisions, that Wall Street and Main Street are intertwined, that you can't have successful securities investing without successful companies to invest in, and you can't have successful companies without motivated engaged workers.

The idea that enriching our wealthiest citizens and corporations, will cause the money to eventually trickle-down to the workers is wrongheaded. Give a rich person a tax break and he will just put the money in the bank. In a world of global capital flows, such a miniscule increase in global savings will have little to no impact on the general American economy.

But give the average American the opportunity to work for a fair wage, with the chance for personal growth and advancement and the ability to give his children a superior education, and the effects on economic growth will be tremendous. Getting the underemployed working again and removing artificial ceilings to advancement will have an immediate impact on the economy, but the biggest long-term economic benefit will be the ability of the sons and daughters of janitors and carpenters to grow up to be scientists, doctors, and successful business executives.

America is at the crossroads of two very different paths in her development. The low road is one of greed, insider information, corrupt deal making, and governing that only favors the elite. The high road is one of openness, economic opportunity, and compassion for the less fortunate. Our economic prosperity depends on our taking the right path. Future generations of Americans will know whether we made the right choice or not.

One of those who came before Obama, who also spoke about opportunity and justice as the cornerstones of any successful and prosperous economic system, was Robert Kennedy, often remembered as one of our greatest speakers. People of all races, creeds, ages, and genders were drawn to him. They thought he spoke honestly and from the heart.

It is hard to forget the extemporaneous words of wisdom he spoke to an anxious crowd in inner-city Indianapolis on the night of April 4, 1968, just after Martin Luther King was killed in Memphis. A largely black crowd had waited an hour to hear the presidential candidate speak, and many in the crowd had not heard the news of King's death. Kennedy had been warned not to go by the city's police chief.

> For those of you who are black and are tempted to be filled with hatred and distrust at the injustice of such an act, against all white people, I can only say that I feel in my own heart the same kind of feeling. I had a member of my family killed, but he was killed by a white man. . . .
>
> My favorite poet was Aeschylus. He wrote: "In our sleep, pain which cannot forget falls drop by drop upon the heart until, in our own despair, against our will, comes wisdom through the awful grace of God."
>
> What we need in the United States is not division; what we need in the United States is not hatred; what we need in the United States is not violence or lawlessness; but love and wisdom, and compassion toward one another, and a feeling of justice toward those who still suffer within our country, whether they be white or they be black.[18]

Of course, to describe Bobby Kennedy as a great speaker betrays his legacy. It would be like saying that Beethoven was a piano player, or that Michelangelo painted ceilings. Are speeches merely words? Yes, great political speeches are made of words, but they convey great ideas. Great speeches impart wisdom. They express feelings that the audience shares, but has been unable to articulate before into words. They speak truth. They call upon the better angels of our nature to reaffirm our most basic human instincts of compassion, love and empathy. And they can be beautiful.

And where do the words come from? Assembled in the mind, they must be creations of the heart. They come from the speaker's life experiences.

Bobby Kennedy went through an enormous transformation in his life. He went from being the son of a multimillionaire father, to the hotheaded younger brother who would do anything to protect his president, to a thoughtful, calm visionary who understood our nation, our people and its greatness, and began to speak out for the disenfranchised. He was not afraid of facing injustice, in fact he went in search of it, from the wrath-filled lettuce fields of California, to the poverty-stricken coal mining towns of Appalachia, to our country's blight-ridden inner cities.

As Bobby Kennedy's words illustrate, he was interested in unifying America. He saw the destructive impact that petty infighting was causing this great nation. He believed that the country and its people would be better off if we found ways to cooperate and get along. But he also felt that it was the right thing to do. Hatred is inherently wrong. Once we learn to like our neighbor, we gain a respect for the person and his or her views and, hopefully, learn how to listen to positions different than our own on important issues.

1968 was a long time ago. Can any historical parallels be drawn? In 1968, Bobby Kennedy ran for president and opposed a war that had been ongoing for six years and had killed thousands of Americans and tens of thousands of Vietnamese. The sitting president at the time was a Texan who was greatly disliked for his support of the war and for his quickness to use unilateral military force and bombing, rather than negotiation, to deal with conflicts. The eventual winner of that election campaign, a Republican who has since been accused by his fellow party members of not being a true conservative, ran on a platform of fear. He convinced Americans that winning a small civil war in a Third World country halfway around the world was the key to defeating an ideology—communism, that he said—which threatened our great nation and the world. The war continued on for seven more long years before we eventually pulled out, with 58,000 Americans dead and no favorable resolution to the conflict.

At home, Kennedy made the great struggle for civil rights and against injustice that others had begun his own. The economy was performing acceptably, but much of it was due to excessive war spending and a government that was incapable of staying within budget. The overall economy was growing, but large groups of our citizens were not participating in that growth and prosperity. Kennedy reached out to people to assure them that their lives were important, that they deserved the same human rights and dignity as everyone else.

Kennedy recognized that the powerful had a disproportionate voice in Washington. He wrote, "The essential humanity of men can be protected and preserved only where government must answer—not just to the wealthy, not just to those of a particular religion, or a particular race, but to all its people."[19]

One does not typically think of Bobby Kennedy as a leading thinker on economics, but he recognized that our economy depended, to a great degree, on a firm foundation of institutions and principles that were greater than the economy itself. He saw that for this country to prosper we all had to cooperate and work together. He gave one of the most powerful speeches on the American economic system ever to the Commonwealth Club of California on January 4, 1968, just five months before his death. Here is one excerpt:

> Truly we have a great gross national product, almost $800 billion, but can that be the criterion by which we judge this country? Is it enough? For the gross national product counts air pollution and cigarette advertising and ambulances to clear our highways of carnage. It counts special

locks for our doors and jails for the people who break them. It counts Whitman's rifle and Speck's knife and television programs, which glorify violence in order to sell toys to our children. And the gross national product, the gross national product does not allow for the health of our children, the quality of their education, the joy of their play. It is indifferent to the decency of our factories and the safety of our streets alike. It does not include the beauty of our poetry or the strength of our marriages, the intelligence of our public debate or the integrity of our public officials. It measures neither wit nor courage, neither our wisdom nor our learning, neither our compassion nor our duty to our country. It measures everything, in short, except that which makes life worthwhile, and it can tell us everything about America, except why we are proud to be Americans.[20]

In addition to believing that America overemphasized economic measures in judging the greatness of our country, Kennedy suggested that the very measurements we use are inadequate. The Gross Domestic Product (GDP) includes many things it should not, and excludes other considerations that are essential to understanding the true health and prosperity of our nation.

You cannot miss that Kennedy refers to our GDP as being $800 billion. Today, it is over $14 trillion, or approximately $2.3 trillion in Kennedy's constant uninflated 1968 dollars.[21] But amplifying Kennedy's point, what does this number include? It seems that there are a large number of activities included in our economic numbers today that are not actually productive, but are undertaken solely to correct problems resulting from our own haphazard economic development. For example, included in our GDP is approximately $500 billion spent on environmental equipment and processes that actually do nothing more than attempt to return our ecologic system back to the state it was in before we started industrial production.[22]

I'm not saying that we don't appreciate clean air, only that we already had it before we started polluting. We shouldn't say that cleaning up pollution is unproductive, but it is a funny kind of productivity, since all we are doing is getting back something we already had: clean air and water, and a healthy planet.

There are many, many examples like this in our current economy. Sixteen percent of our GDP goes to healthcare,[23] but how many of our doctor visits and psychiatrist sessions are a direct result of the unhealthy lifestyles caused by the pressures and time constraints of our highly productive world? We develop expensive defense systems for our nations protection, sell them to our supposed friends around the world, then end up spending even more to develop more sophisticated weapons when these friends turn on us. We work in great cities that require our food, our apparel, and our toys to be shipped to us over great distances; our work puts us on carbon-emitting flights around the world; and for vacation, we spend enormous amounts of money trying to recreate the simpler existence we enjoyed in our rural hometowns before we ever decided to embark on this path to development.

Today, much of our reported GDP is composed of three things: 1) fixing mistakes we have made in the past, such as cleaning up pollution, 2) over-consumption based on borrowing from future generations, and 3) those activities that have only recently begun to be counted and reported as production. For example, a mother that used to stay at home to do the housework and raise the children for free, may now decide to go to work, increasing the GDP with her salary, but also expanding it by the amount she now has to pay for child care, tutors, fast food, house cleaning, lawn care, commuting to work, and elderly care for her parents—tasks she used to do for free. Like the pigs in *Animal Farm*,[24] our government tells us we are better off measured in GDP terms; it's no wonder we're having increasing difficulty seeing how this is so.

A very large portion of our GDP consists of increasingly expensive attempts to differentiate ourselves from our friends and neighbors to satisfy our desire for status. A $14,000 Corolla (or a used $3,500 Chevy) will take you to the same places as a $120,000 Hummer, but not in quite as much style. Our drive for higher status is temporarily satisfied on the trip, but we may not necessarily be any better off once we get there. Many families today choose to live in 12,000 square foot McMansions rather than more modest 1,500 to 2,000 square foot homes. Building these monstrosities dramatically increases GDP, but it is unclear whether productivity or well-being has increased much at all. An economist may argue that since someone purchased the larger home in the free market under no coercion, they must value it and it must reflect greater well-being, but this ignores the fact that society and the media encourage ever greater consumption in our nation.

Many Americans today may be feeling a certain hollowness and emptiness after constantly chasing higher earnings and greater pay, only to find that there is a limit to the amount of happiness that money can buy. There has to be a large number of middle-aged Americans out there who, having reached a material definition of success, are asking themselves, "Is that all there is?"

Our country also likes to focus on stock market levels and stock indices as a measure of how prosperous the country is. But the stock market measures prosperity from only one perspective, that of the business owner. The dilemma of capitalism is that it tries to maximize profit, but the biggest detriment to profit is workers' wages. Thus, as workers' wages decline, corporate profits increase, and the stock market increases. When we hear that the stock market went up in value by $1 billion, we honestly don't know whether the pie expanded and the country is worth $1 billion more, or whether the pie has been sliced differently and instead $1 billion of value has been shifted from the workers to the owners. Globalization and the glut of underemployed workers in the world, the decline of unions, and the failure of the minimum wage to keep up with inflation, immigration, and outsourcing have all put pressure on the wages and benefits of the average American worker. We applaud ourselves that the Dow Jones average has increased from 2,000 to 12,000 over the last twenty-five years—an increase in value in real dollar terms of approximately $3 trillion—but a simple arithmetic exercise shows that this could have been accomplished by reducing the average worker's pay by $2.00 to $3.00 an hour rather than inventing new products or providing a new and better service to the consumer. Capitalism is based on the assumption that, in aggregate, increasing profits are good for a company and a country, but this presumption has to be reevaluated in a global world where American companies fire American workers and hire foreign workers.

In his speech to the Commonwealth Club, Kennedy made the following observations about foreign policy:

> Beyond our borders, we have become the greatest force in the world. Some have even spoken of us as the new imperial power. Even if we should desire such a role, it is no longer possible, as the history of the last twenty years has so unmistakably shown. The day has passed when a country can successfully rule distant lands by force. The issue for us is whether we will live as an island in the midst of a hostile world community or whether we will be joined with other independent nations in search of common goals. We must understand this, because so much depends on what is going to happen in the future as to whether this concept is clear to us. Other countries will associate themselves with us, not because they will be forced to, but because they find in our acts and in our policies a common interest and an understanding of their own ideals and their own aspirations; an understanding of the values that they can respect and admire; an understanding of the values that they can strive to emulate . . . .
>
> For two hundred years, America has meant a vision of national independence and personal freedom and justice

between men. But whether it will continue to mean this will depend on the answers to difficult and complex problems. It will depend on whether we sit content in our storehouses, dieting while others starve, buying eight million new cars a year while most of the world goes without shoes. . . . It will depend on whether we can halt and can reverse the tide of ever greater centralization in Washington and return the power to the American people in their local communities. It will depend on whether we can turn the private genius of industry to the service of great public ends. . . . It will depend on whether we still hold, as the framers proclaimed, a decent respect for the opinions of mankind, or whether we will act as if no other nations existed, flaunting our power and flaunting our wealth against the judgment and desires of neutrals and allies alike.[25]

Ted Kennedy gave the eulogy for his brother at St. Patrick's Cathedral in New York. I quote, "My brother need not be idealized or enlarged in death beyond what he was in life, to be remembered simply as a good and decent man, who saw wrong and tried to right it, saw suffering and tried to heal it, saw war and tried to stop it . . . [He said,] Some men see things as they are and say 'Why?' I dream things that never were and say, 'Why not?'"[26]

We miss him very much.

> *Anybody here seen my old friend Bobby?*
> *Can you tell me where he's gone?*
> *I thought I saw him walkin' up over the hill*
> *With Abraham, Martin, and John.*[27]

Chapter One

ECONOMIC JUSTICE

*. . . we gather to affirm the greatness of our Nation—
not because of the height of our skyscrapers, or the
power of our military, or the size of our economy. Our
pride is based on a very simple premise, summed up
in a declaration made over two hundred years ago:*

*"We hold these truths to be self-evident, that all
men are created equal, that they are endowed by their
Creator with certain inalienable rights, that among
these are Life, Liberty and the pursuit of Happiness."*

*That is the true genius of America, a faith—a
faith in simple dreams, an insistence on small miracles; that we can tuck in our children at night and
know that they are fed and clothed and safe from
harm; that we can say what we think, write what we
think, without hearing a sudden knock on the door;
that we can have an idea and start our own business
without paying a bribe; that we can participate in the
political process without fear of retribution, and that
our votes will be counted—at least most of the time.*[1]

These words are from Barack Obama's major economic policy
speech at the General Motors Assembly Plant in Janesville, Wis-
consin on February 13, 2008.[2] It was a different kind of economic
speech than we are used to hearing from our presidential candidates. It had a completely different focus than the macroeconomic
issues we are used to hearing discussed in Washington. Obama did
not speak about the government deficit, or our trade with China, or
the ballooning government debt, or where the stock market was
going, or about intellectual property rights for corporations, or

about tax cuts for the wealthy. Rather, he focused his remarks on what, for him, is the most pressing need today in America, the need for economic justice. He did not describe a narrow definition of justice that involved simply handing out money to the poor. Rather, he attempted to make us realize how unjust the current system is, and the simple things that can be done to make it more fair. As we shall see, fairness and justice are extremely important concepts in keeping an economy prosperous and growing, because without them, it is difficult to keep economic participants, especially workers and investors, motivated. Here is an excerpt from the Obama speech that day:

> It's a Washington where George Bush hands out billions in tax cuts year after year to the biggest corporations and the wealthiest few who don't need them and don't ask for them—tax breaks that are mortgaging our children's future on a mountain of debt; tax breaks that could've gone into the pockets of the working families who needed them most.
>
> A Washington where decades of trade deals like NAFTA and China have been signed with plenty of protections for corporations and their profits, but none for our environment or our workers who've seen factories shut their doors and millions of jobs disappear; workers whose right to organize and unionize has been under assault for the last eight years . . .
>
> And it's a Washington that has thrown open its doors to lobbyists and special interests who've riddled our tax code with loopholes that let corporations avoid paying their taxes while you're paying more. They've been allowed to write an energy policy that's keeping us addicted to oil when there are families choosing between gas and groceries. They've used money and influence to kill health care reform at a time when half of all bankruptcies are

caused by medical bills, and then they've rigged our bank-ruptcy laws to make it harder to climb out of debt . . .

This is what's been happening in Washington at a time when we have greater income disparity in this country than we've seen since the first year of the Great Depression. . . . And it's a time when one in eight Americans now lives in abject poverty right here in the richest nation on Earth.[3]

This book, and to a great degree, much of Barack Obama's platform for America, is about a singular issue, economic justice.[4] The word "economic" is broadly defined to include all those matters that affect the ability to earn a livelihood, become a productive member of society, and invest for your family's future. But the key word is justice.

If we examine possible solutions to the major problems facing our nation from the simple perspective of trying to achieve justice, it is much easier to understand the "right" direction to take.

Why the pursuit of justice, rather than more immediate and conventional goals, such as maximizing personal or national wealth, the state's power, economic advantage and military might, should be our nation's organizing principle is a deeply philosophical question. With apologies to Aristotle and Plato, and to philosophers who have taken thousands of years to study it, let us take two or three pages here to give an overly simplified, and certainly incomplete, explanation so we can better understand the issue.

Justice is mostly about fairness. People wish to be treated fairly. If they are asked to compete in school or at work, they hope it will be on a level playing field where all have an equal opportunity to demonstrate their ability. Justice is a primary organizing principle of successful societies, governments, and economies because, first, we all wish to be treated fairly and to be judged on our own merits; and second, it turns out that just societies are typically much more successful than unjust ones.

Obama says, ". . . we have always been in a constant balancing act between self-interest and community, markets and democracy, the concentration of wealth and power and the opening up of opportunity. We've lost that balance in Washington, I think."[5]

Obama's writings suggest that an emphasis on societal justice derives from our common belief in the sanctity of the individual spirit and the inherent equality of all individuals. He writes, ". . . at the core of the American experience are a set of ideals that continue to stir our collective conscience; a common set of values that bind us together despite our differences; a running thread of hope that makes our improbable experiment in democracy work."[6]

We believe individuals should be as free as possible to pursue their life goals, as these goals and aspirations define better than anything else what makes up an individual. And Obama believes all individuals should have equal opportunity to achieve their objectives. It is this equal treatment of all individuals that forms the foundation of a just society.

In Obama's words, "At its most elemental level, we understand our liberty in a negative sense. As a general rule we believe in the right to be left alone, and are suspicious of those—whether Big Brother or nosy neighbors—who want to meddle in our business. But we understand our liberty in a more positive sense as well, in the idea of opportunity and a subsidiary of values that help realize opportunity—all those homespun virtues that Benjamin Franklin first popularized. . . . But these values also express a broader confidence that so long as individual men and women are free to pursue their own interests, society as a whole will prosper."[7]

Certainly, if we believed that people and their chosen life paths were not equal, we would not adopt a system that treated everybody justly and fairly. In such a world, it would make much more sense to favor those who were valued more by society, who were more equal, so to speak. If we value the life prospects of a wealthy child more than a poor child, then we should not be just, we should create a system that provides undue benefits to the wealthy child to maximize the probability he'll attain his life goals, even if the poor family's child has to suffer. If we value the life prospects of a white child more than a black child, we should not be just, for by doing so we run the risk that the less equal black child will somehow outperform the more equal white. If we value the life prospects of a boy child more than a girl child, we should not act justly, as we would never want to give the girl the same chance at success as the boy.

But, like Obama, if we value every child, if we hold dear every life, if we want to hear every American story, and if we want to give all the opportunity to excel, then we will value justice over everything. Of course, we have all heard Obama speak about hope. Obama has written an entire book on the subject.[8] What is hope? Hope is nothing more than every individual reaching and striving to achieve his or her goals, and a society reaching and striving to be just and fair so that all may have the opportunity to do so.

As Obama says, "If anything, what struck me was just how modest people's hopes were, and how much of what they believe seemed to hold constant across race, region, religion, and class. Most of them thought that anybody willing to work should be able to find a job that paid a living wage. They figured that people shouldn't have to file for bankruptcy because they got sick. They believed that every child should have a genuinely good education . . . they wanted to be safe, from criminals and from terrorists; they wanted clean air, clean water, and time with their kids and when they got old, they wanted to be able to retire with some dignity and respect."[9]

That is why Obama speaks to the power of bottom-up economics as opposed to trickle-down economic theory. The trickle-down economic theory says that we should give those at the top more, and they will start and expand businesses and provide jobs and income for all. This is not a theory; it is propaganda put out by a Congress controlled by the wealthy to try to justify giving fully one third of the Bush tax cuts to the top 1 percent of earners in America.[10] The money did not go to start businesses and create jobs, it went into wealthy people's savings accounts. They didn't need our money if they wanted to start or expand a business. The top 1 percent of the country's earners already controlled 40 percent of the country's financial assets.[11] In a world where capital flows globally over the Internet in a second, it is laughable that somehow more good business ideas would be funded here if we gave our wealthiest citizens another windfall profit.

The power of bottom-up economics, according to Obama, is that it is an economically just system that encourages everyone to work hard, to educate themselves, and to be their most productive, because it fairly rewards those who do so. A white man, a black man, a woman, an Arab, a Jew, a Muslim, and yes, even a poor person, all have the same opportunities, and thus all are equally motivated to excel, because they know the system will treat them fairly and reward their hard work and effort.

Obama writes, "It taught me that ordinary people can do extraordinary things when given the chance. Change does not happen from the top down, but from the bottom-up, because the American people stand ready for change. . . . Just like we need bottom-up politics, we need bottom-up economics. We need to think about working people."[12]

To those who argue that wealth maximization is an admirable personal as well as national goal, it is important to remember that almost all who think this way would not be willing to sacrifice justice to attain wealth. Very few would rob their neighbor in order to maximize their own wealth, even if they were certain they could get away with it. When someone says they wish to maximize their wealth, or even the wealth of their nation, it is understood that such activity will be subject to the underlying principles of justice and fairness. For most, the achievement of wealth and power has no value if attained in unjust ways.

Why do we as individuals value justice so highly? As Obama says, we realize we are all in this together. We are our brother's keepers. We are our sister's keepers. No man is an island. And so, in determining how societal and governmental rules will dictate our behavior toward others, we arrived at a simple formulation that says we will treat others like we wish to be treated—a simple but effective formulation of what justice involves.

Obama also believes there is a higher moral purpose to life, even in our economic lives. He is not satisfied with an economy and society that is based solely on individual wealth maximization. He understands the tenets of Adam Smith's invisible hand, in which each of us pursuing our own goals and objectives through a market-based economy can benefit the entire society. But he also recognizes that there are more fundamental issues and problems that cannot be solved by individual participants operating in a free market economy, but that we as a society, typically through government, must address. He writes, "That is one of the things that makes me a Democrat, I suppose—this idea that our communal values, our sense of mutual responsibility and social solidarity, should express themselves not just in the church or the mosque or the synagogue; not just on the blocks were we live, in the places where we were, or within our own family; but also through our government."[13]

Obama believes that economic justice is the most important of these. He describes how the future will look if nothing is done: "It will mean a nation even more stratified economically and socially than it currently is: one in which an increasingly prosperous knowledge class, living in exclusive enclaves, will be able to purchase whatever they want on the marketplace—private schools, private healthcare, private security, and private jets—while a growing number of their fellow citizens are consigned to low-paying service jobs, vulnerable to dislocation, pressed to work longer hours, depending on an underfunded, overburdened, and underperforming public sector for their health care, retirement, and their children's educations."[14]

Free markets are many things, but they cannot claim to be moral. Not that they are necessarily immoral; amoral is a better description. Properly regulated free markets should end up rewarding hard work and effort, dedication, intellect, knowledge, and will provide products and services of value to others. Obama, like Bobby Kennedy before him, realizes that markets, unlike humans, cannot step outside themselves to see when they are doing damage to our social fabric, our environment, and our nation's standing in the world, or judge the fairness and justice of their harsh profit-oriented bottom line on families and the poor. Only humans can see beyond the free market to judge whether it is satisfying larger societal goals. But we aren't the only animals with complex sets of values. Other animals do not depend solely on the survival of the fittest, but also have communal families and clans, methods of encouraging cooperation with others, and societal rules.

The major economic problems our country faces today are those which, by definition, the free market acting alone couldn't solve. If they could have been solved by a profit-driven market, someone would have done so, and gotten rich. For example, Obama points out, markets often ignore poverty because the poor don't have enough dollars (i.e., economic votes) to get the markets to understand what their needs are. Obama says that solutions to problems like Social Security and Medicare confuse the market because the prime elderly beneficiary is separated from the much younger premium payer by generations, an intergenerational problem free markets have difficulty dealing with. Obama describes the free market approach thusly: "If we free employers of any obligations to their workers and dismantle what's left of the New Deal, government-run, social insurance programs, then the magic of the marketplace will take care of the rest." Clearly, it won't.[15]

The environment and global warming are externalities to an efficient free market; supply and demand-determined pricing clears the marketplace without even considering the environmental consequences. A free market could never determine what percentage of taxes the rich and poor should pay. And foreign policy issues, especially issues of war and peace, should never be determined by

free market participants like defense contractors, who stand to benefit if our nation goes to war. Obama believes that many of the
highly complex global problems we face require cooperation and
the collective action of not only our citizens, but the citizens of the
world—that the guiding principle of such an effort should be economic justice. Such a cooperative group effort is beyond the scope
of the utility-maximizing, egocentric, free market-oriented individual participant. But Obama spends a great deal of his time
talking about how a strong leader can encourage cooperation
among the citizenry.

As Obama clearly understands, it turns out that it is good for
your economy to be just. Daron Acemoglu, the MIT professor who
recently won the award for being the top economist in America
under the age of forty, wrote a brilliant paper that attempts to show
why the rich countries of the world are rich, and why the poor
countries of the world are poor.[16] He is not the first to attempt an
explanation for this seemingly innocent question. Hundreds of
other researchers have proposed models examining thousands of
current policy variables, including hundreds of government and
macroeconomic statistics, and none has uncovered the true underlying cause for the disparity in wealth among the nations of the
world.

Acemoglu showed empirically that countries such as the United
States, Australia, and Canada that have very prosperous and
vibrant economies today were also those countries in which the ini-
tial colonizers, the British, decided to settle and raise their families
hundreds of years ago. Conversely, those former European colonies
in Africa and South America which continue to struggle today
economically were historically those countries that, due mostly to
the hot climate and related disease, were inhospitable to the colonizers. Thus, the colonizers, rather than settling their families
there, extracted natural resources and did some trading with the
native peoples, but primarily never made the colonies their home
and never settled there in as large numbers.[17]

This should shock you. What Acemoglu is saying is that to a great degree the economic success of your country today was not determined by your president's economic policies last year, nor by your government's laws and statutes passed over the last few decades. Rather, the best predictor of how well your country is doing today was established some 400 years ago when it was colonized.

Acemoglu believes that the reason that those countries in which the colonizers settled developed faster is that the colonizers brought with them valuable institutions. Acemoglu does not reveal which of these economic-friendly institutions were most important, but it appears, based on empirical work by Richard Roll of UCLA and myself,[18] that they include property rights, the rule of law, and also such important political institutions as the democratic vote, civil liberties, and a free press—essentially the foundations for a democratic free-market economy. We were able to demonstrate empirically that the existence of democratic institutions like the vote and a free press did indeed lead to greater economic prosperity in a country.

It is possible to view Acemoglu's work at an even more fundamental level. Maybe it wasn't just the British court system, contract law, and monetary system that we Americans inherited. Maybe it was the sense that these institutions the British brought with them encompassed an understanding born of the Enlightenment, namely a respect for all individuals, a belief that kings should not rule over men, and a deep abiding insistence on justice.

The colonizers developed more just and fair governmental and economic systems in the countries they decided to settle in as opposed to those from which they merely extracted natural resources. Why? Isn't the answer obvious? In the countries where they would live, they were making rules by which they themselves and their children would have to abide by. They wanted to be assured that their children would be treated fairly, with the opportunity to achieve their dreams that a just society would provide.

Under this theory, it was not only what we inherited from the British that was important. It was also what we revolted against—namely, that one man might rule over others, that one class should be favored over others and that your heritage and your parents should determine your life's opportunities more than your life's accomplishments and your own merit. What is the correlation, today, between those countries that are the most economically just and their prosperity? That study hasn't been done yet.

Obama is a descendant of Kenya, and is very aware of the unjust governmental practices inherited from the colonial British. He saw his father's successful career as a diplomat and finance expert in Kenya evaporate because his father would not support an unjust dictator. As a youth Obama moved to Indonesia, another former colony, and watched again as his father-in-law's career was virtually destroyed because he was at odds with the ruling elite.

Obama's love for America is embodied in this striking contrast between his father's and father-in-law's experiences and his own success in a land where people are free to pursue their life's goals without interference from the government. Much of Obama's legal career has been devoted to insuring that all Americans enjoy the protection of civil liberties and human rights. Obama's community-organizing work was based on his belief that even the most disadvantaged among us deserve the same rights.

If our country's biggest problems are all partly caused by injustice, there are practical solutions that become more evident once we begin to emphasize justice and fairness.

Let us examine the largest economic marketplaces in the world: our stock markets and our financial markets. Clearly, as is dramatically exhibited during the current financial crisis, all is not well on Wall Street. Our financial markets are in disarray. The cause of the current problem is the housing market collapse,[19] but this is not the first time our markets have been threatened. One can easily connect the dots through a number of financial crises over the last two decades, starting with the leveraged buyout collapse in 1990, the US recession of 1991, the Japanese real estate collapse in 1993, the Mexican peso bailout in 1994, the Thailand crash of 1997, the bankruptcy of Russia in 1998, the bailout of Long Term Credit Corporation in 1999, the bursting of the Internet bubble in 2001, the aforementioned housing crash beginning in 2006, the credit crunch beginning in 2007, and the financial markets' threatened collapse beginning in 2008.[20] In addition, there were fundamental macroeconomic concerns in the country, such as an exploding government debt and a US government incapable of balancing its budget, throughout this period.

What does justice have to do with any of these market dislocations? We have allowed our markets to become extremely unregulated. Obama, a lawyer, understands that regulation is the cornerstone of economic justice. Not the type of stifling bureaucratic regulation that prevents an entrepreneur from starting his own business, but enough regulation to ensure everybody is playing the game by the same rules without inherent unfair advantage.[21]

In financial markets, Obama believes this means enforcing the laws that prohibit the trading of securities based on insider information. Deep liquid security markets requiring the active participation of all investors are impossible if some investors are allowed to trade and profit on the inside information available only to those closest to a company. One can argue that individuals are not a big piece of the trading volume or share ownership on the stock exchanges these days. This may be so, but their retirement savings and pension funds, their insurance premiums, their savings in mutual funds, and 401(k)s are all heavily invested in the stock market. There is no reason why a person, or his pension fund, would want to buy a company's stock from a hedge fund if he knew the reason they were selling was because they had just received non-public bad news from the company itself. No one would.

Expanding on Obama's concerns about fairness and justice in the financial system, one can see that a number of hedge funds have gotten very large and very profitable by constantly beating the market each year. Modern economic theory says this is impossible. Market theory says that, randomly, some people might beat the market each year, but a warning should sound if it is the same people and institutions that are successfully outperforming year in and year out. If it turns out that hedge funds are relying on insider information and unfairly trading with the less well-informed, it could be devastating for the marketplace. Investors and the institutions that represent them could decide to pull out entirely. This happened in 2001 to some degree, when investors concluded that the investment banks were showing favor to their largest institutional clients, and individual investors pulled large amounts of money out of the stock market and place it in an asset they thought they understood better: residential real estate. Of course, homes turned out to be more difficult to value properly than high-tech stocks, and this flood of money into residential real estate became partly responsible for the subsequent housing collapse.

A just financial system has to enforce laws to prevent insider trading. Similarly, Obama believes there is no place in a just financial system for market manipulation. In a speech in New York, he said, ". . . we must remain vigilant and crack down on trading activity that crosses the line to market manipulation. Reports have circulated in recent days that some traders may have intentionally spread rumors that Bear Stearns was in financial distress while making market bets against the company. The SEC should investigate and punish this kind of market manipulation, and report its conclusions to Congress."[22]

Again, some hedge funds today are so large, and concentrate on the trading of so few individual securities, that they represent a large percentage of the overall total daily volume. It would not be surprising to find out that some of them were involved in manipulating some of these thinly traded stocks. Manipulation, like insider trading, is inherently unfair and unjust, because it gives the individual investor a false minor increase in profit, only to be wiped out as a hedge fund sells out of its position. It is a game as old as the Denver penny stock market, and before that, Wall Street speculators in the 1920s like Joe Kennedy, but in the name of fairness it has no place on Wall Street.

Another game hedge funds play that is totally unjust, and that Obama may want to investigate, is that many act as a guarantor or insurer if certain bad events occur in the future. For example, many small hedge funds provide insurance to companies against a possible bankruptcy of the companies whose debt securities they hold. This is accomplished by the hedge funds writing contracts that allow the defaulted bonds to be put to them, or more directly in the credit derivatives market, by collecting annual cash payments in return for a promise to make the investor whole if one of the companies they invest in goes bankrupt.

The reason why this arm's length transaction is inherently unjust, and should be illegal, is that the small hedge funds and small monoline insurance companies are not of substantial enough size and do not have a significant enough capital base to honor these guarantees and promises if things go badly in the future. Insurance has no value if the insuring party goes bankrupt before it can reimburse you for your loss. Real insurance companies, who are in this business full-time, are heavily regulated by state and federal authorities for exactly this reason. Hedge fund managers are not stupid. They know they face this risk. But it is a risk that will only occur under a very low probability state of future circumstances. The hedge fund is comfortable collecting the current premiums and enriching themselves with the knowledge that if things do turn badly they can always fold up their hedge fund, head to the elevators, get to their jets waiting at the airport, and most likely, be back in business in a year with a new fund, in a new country if need be.

Finally, many companies on Wall Street are dramatically over-leveraged with debt. Obama has not specifically mentioned this in his remarks to date, but he would be wise to focus on it as it causes great volatility to our economy. Commercial banks, which traditionally have been leveraged at less than $10.00 of debt for every one dollar of equity capital, now report debt leverage of more than sixteen to one, and that is before including off-balance sheet debt, which can drive their leverage up to more than twenty-five to one. Hedge funds can be leveraged as much as they want, as they are almost completely unregulated, but the recent bankruptcy of Carlyle Capital, one of the major hedge funds investing in mortgage securities, showed that it was leveraged thirty-two to one. Investment banks, unregulated with regard to capital requirements and leverage ratios, are leveraged approximately twenty to one, although Bear Stearns, before it was forced to sell to J.P. Morgan in a Federal Reserve bailout, was leveraged thirty-two to one.[23]

What does this have to do with justice? Isn't this just good business? Aren't returns to the shareholders maximized by utilizing the greatest amount of available debt leverage? Again, one of the tenets of a just financial system is that contracts will be honored. When leverage at financial institutions gets this large, it is an indication that executives have placed their own stock option compensation ahead of the primacy of honoring contracts with their customers. At this degree of leverage, by definition, managers are saying that they are willing to risk bankruptcy and the violation of all of their existing business contracts with investors and debt holders just to improve their own financial compensation. That is unjust.

Unfair practices are not restricted solely to Wall Street in the business community. Obama believes that corporate America on Main Street, in addition to Wall Street, is guilty of one of the most unjust practices that is doing the greatest harm to our nation, namely, bribing our public officials with campaign donations and hiring lobbyists to press their own agendas instead of those in the public's common interest. Obama knows that undue corporate influence and their "special interest" in Washington is another of the primary causes of many of the major problems this country faces. The concept that a corporation is a "person" entitled to the rights of persons, such as the right to seek an audience with elected officials, violates any conception of what the founding fathers meant by individual rights. There is nothing human or individual about a corporation. It is a fabricated legal entity existing only in the files of the secretary of state of Delaware. It is completely unjust to all Americans for corporations to be treated as persons. If GM has a political position it supports, let it convince its employees to vote for it. The only real persons inside GM are the people who work there.

Even if you agree that corporations have the rights of persons, and have the right to pursue their corporate business purposes with our elected representatives, there can be no justification for why their concerns should count more than those of the average citizen. Obama believes such an assumption violates our basic premise of equal treatment. It has to be unjust that campaign contributions dominate our elections, because it violates the theory of one man one vote—that each of our votes should be weighed equally, and that we should have equal access to our elected representatives under the law. Having more money, especially if it's corporate money, should not allow you greater access to our elected representatives. You would have to be quite naïve to think that all that money is just buying access. There is no for-profit corporation that would pay good money just for access. They are getting something in return; in fact, they are getting trillions of dollars of value in return for making hundreds of millions of dollars of donations and lobbying investments.

Obama has also identified another area of injustice in our economic system: the unjust power of monopolies, collusion among supposed competitors, and the ensuing damage both to consumers and entrepreneurs. Obama has spoken directly about his concerns that the healthcare insurance industry may be too concentrated, with the top two competitors controlling one third of the entire market nationally. Obama adds, "The market alone can't solve our healthcare woes—in part because the market has proven incapable of creating large enough insurance pools to keep costs to individuals affordable, in part because healthcare is not like other products or services (when your child gets sick, you don't go shopping for the best bargain)."[24] But, the power of monopolies in America is not limited solely to the healthcare industry.

In our corporate dominated economy, monopolies and collusive behavior between supposed competitors can prevent the proper operation of our markets, distorting true prices and punishing consumers. Why do breakfast cereals sell for $3.95 when they contain less than $0.16 of corn and grain value? How do you think Coca-Cola products, like Coke, Diet Coke, Cherry Coke, Caffeine Free Cherry Coke, and so on came to take up an entire aisle in the supermarket, pushing smaller brands off the shelf into oblivion? Why do cable television companies charge hundreds of dollars a month for a service that costs them tens of dollars per customer to build out? Why do most credit cards charge the same exorbitant interest rates? How do most banks get away charging ridiculous monthly fees and service charges? Why is it illegal to buy a new car on the Internet if you want to avoid the 30 percent overhead cost and hassle of going to a dealer? Why do you need a license to cut hair? Why does an engineer need education certificates and degrees to teach high school math? Why is annual tuition approximately the same at all the top universities? How can Microsoft afford to have such poor customer service and ignore improving their operations and applications software that have 98 percent market shares? Why does Lowe's keep prices low in a community until they bankrupt the local hardware stores and then raise them? Why are gas prices almost exactly the same in each neighborhood, and why do they increase in exactly the same increments on the same days? Why do short flights to small towns cost more than long flights between big cities? Why are all banks quick to raise their prime lending rate for their best lending customers quickly when interest rates increase, but very slow to lower them when rates decline? Why does it cost many times more to ship cargo by train if there is just one track and one carrier? Why are so many industries dominated by two or three "market leaders" whose combined market shares often exceed 40 to 50 percent of the market, and who decide never to have price wars, and who match each other's price increases dollar for dollar? Why do farmers have to accept a low price for their cattle or hogs from a regionally dominant pork or meat processor who has bought up all the local competition, and is now the only game in town?

No economist, when speaking about properly functioning free markets, includes possible manipulation of those markets by monopolies as an acceptable practice. There has never been a calculation of the damage monopolies do to our society in dollar terms, but they overcharge consumers trillions of dollars a year for products and services, constrain competition, and limit innovation in their industries. Monopolies, are of course, illegal. But the Bush administration and the Justice Department have been very slow in bringing any monopoly or collusion action against any American company. In colluding to set prices, competitors violate the first economic assumption of markets, that the players are independent and separate and working solely for their own independent objectives. Collusion is dishonest, and it is unjust.

From an individual's perspective, economic justice is paramount. It is no coincidence that a black man like Obama is leading this charge. His life is a testimony to the importance of economic justice. His grandfather is Muslim, so Obama knows about religious persecution. His father is from Kenya, a country whose corruption of its government and business community has held back economic development for decades. As a single mom, his mother raised him under financial duress, including receiving government food stamps when times were tough. As a youngster, Obama lived in Indonesia, a world leader for decades in government-condoned nepotism and government-supported monopoly power. Upon graduating from college, Obama worked as a community organizer with the poor and dispossessed of Chicago, fighting for human rights for the poor, which an economic system does not automatically provide. After graduating from Harvard Law School, Obama worked as a civil rights attorney fighting for those whose human rights had been ignored by the system, and as an academic instructor and constitutional scholar.[25]

Obama's knowledge of the Constitution is not just academic. One can hear in his speeches and in his words a deep love for the principles of justice, fairness and equality that the founding fathers were intent on introducing to these shores. His work in the Illinois Senate and in the US Senate has been dedicated to improving the lot of those forgotten by the system and to make the operations of the Senate more transparent, ethical, and yes, just.

While racism and prejudice are fundamental concerns of any justice system, they obviously also violate any concept of economic justice. Bias and prejudice in the workplace prevent individuals from acquiring jobs they qualify for, getting promotions they deserve, and providing the incomes necessary to give their children the educational and growth opportunities they deserve.

The poor, the disenfranchised, the young, minorities, Jews, and Gentiles alike have all been drawn to Obama's message. It is a universal message. But it is not a message solely for the disadvantaged as much as it is also for the ears of the elites and the well off. Obama has been careful in his campaign not to point fingers or assign blame for the problems we face. He really does not want to start class warfare. His solutions are not simple transfers from the wealthy to the afflicted. He wishes to unite us all in an effort to solve our problems collectively. He speaks of collective redemption. Some view him as a deliverer of sorts, as he tries to deliver the disadvantaged and the working poor to the promised land, but it will also be the wealthy and well-to-do that end up getting delivered, back to their fundamental beliefs in justice and fairness for all.

Injustice is not limited only to the corporate sphere. Our government itself is ripe with harsh stories of injustice. When a corporation illegally offers a bribe to an elected official, the elected official is equally to blame for accepting it. To some extent, the elected representative is even more to blame, because his chosen profession is public service. While the businessman may have been cheating in offering a bribe, at least his intention was to help his shareholders, which is his stated primary goal. The elected representative violates his oath of office by accepting money and ignoring his constituents' needs.

Earmarks are unjust because they take hard earned taxpayer money and give it to special interests for mostly unproductive purposes. For elected officials to do the government's business in secret is also wrong. Non-public disclosure encourages agreements that are not always in the public's best interest. Obama understands that shining a bright light on government activities is the best way to ensure that lawmakers keep the public interest at heart. He has suggested holding frequent town hall meetings with government representatives on the Internet,[26] and he would be well advised to encourage much of his administration's business, as well as congressional deliberations, to be televised on C-SPAN to prevent secret dealings that harm the people.

There was a growing sense of the injustice between workers in the private sector and government employees. Workers in private industry have seen no real increase in their wages after accounting for inflation for over three decades. During this period their healthcare benefits have been scaled back, and the percentage of them that have defined benefit pension plans guaranteeing them a satisfactory retirement income has declined from 60 to 10 percent. During the same period, many local and federal government employees, from the local fireman or policeman to the DMV employee, from Washington bureaucrats and politicians to the men and women who carry the mail and collect the garbage, have preserved their health and pension benefits, and their wages have done a much better job of keeping up with inflation. They have not suffered from globalization through increased competition, they don't face as great a threat from outsourcing, and they haven't had their jobs shipped overseas.

The unintended result now amounts to an injustice of major proportions. They call it public service. They are known as public servants. And yet the average American working in the private sector earns $26.09 an hour, while the average government employee in America earns close to $39.50 an hour in total compensation, including benefits.[27]

Many local municipalities are going to have very serious financial problems over the next decade. For years, they have promised their employees generous retirement healthcare and pension benefits that are going to be enormously difficult to fund. Many teachers, firemen, policemen and municipal workers can retire as early as age forty, with twenty years of service and guarantees of half their salary in pensions. Many municipal and state employees can choose to retire in their forties and early fifties, receive their pension, and then take jobs in the private sector. It isn't fair to hardworking American taxpayers, who in the aggregate are the employers of all public employees, that they are disadvantaged at both ends of things—as underpaid employees in the private sector earning less than government employees, and as overburdened employers who must fund the pensions and salaries of the government employees whose pay has kept pace with inflation better than their own has.

Obama believes that many of our nation's economic problems today result from our having strayed from the principles our founding fathers left us. He thinks that reintroducing the principles of liberty, freedom, opportunity, equality, and, indeed, justice, will allow our nation to find its way out of our current crisis, solve our most recalcitrant problems, and re-orient our economy toward prosperity and growth, our government toward honesty and effectiveness, and our nation back on the road to greatness.

Chapter Two

ECONOMIC OPPORTUNITY

I'm not talking about blind optimism here—the almost willful ignorance that thinks unemployment will go away if we just don't think about it, or the health care crisis will solve itself if we just ignore it. That's not what I'm talking about. I'm talking about something more substantial. It's the hope of slaves sitting around a fire singing freedom songs; the hope of immigrants setting out for distant shores; the hope of a young naval lieutenant bravely patrolling the Mekong Delta; the hope of a millworker's son who dares to defy the odds; the hope of a skinny kid with a funny name who believes that America has a place for him, too. Hope—Hope in the face of difficulty. Hope in the face of uncertainty. The audacity of hope![1]

Many of us remember these striking words that a young senator-to-be gave as the keynote speaker at the 2004 Democratic Nominating Convention. If there is one word associated with Barack Obama, from all of his campaigns, speeches and books, it would have to be hope. From an economic perspective, the word hope easily translates into economic opportunity. Without economic opportunity, there is no hope. In the developing world, aid organizations try to "provide" healthcare, shelter, food, training, schools, and even proper elections, but without economic opportunity, without jobs, the people are doomed to suffer in poverty. Once people have economic opportunity and jobs, they can buy their own damn food, shelter and healthcare. And their dignity will be preserved.

If you ever visit a small town in the middle of America, and you wake up early enough, you will see something truly amazing. At 5:00 a.m., lights come on in homes, and people gather newspapers from their front yards and sit down to their first cup of coffee. By 6:00 a.m., fathers and mothers both are in their cars beginning their commutes to their jobs, which sometimes can take more than an hour each way. If you find yourself out walking the dog at such an early hour you won't be able to ignore the long line of traffic and lights feeling their way through the dark as parents begin just another ordinary day in America. They will be home by 7:00 p.m., but incredibly, many of them will head off for a second job, some working until past midnight.

These people are the backbone of America. Without them and their hard work we would have no economy. There would be no Caterpillar stock to trade or invest in, because there would be no Caterpillar company without them. As Obama has said, there would be no Wall Street without Main Street.

But as you watch these hardworking, dedicated people sitting in their cars in the very early light of the morning, one question keeps returning, "Why do they do it? What motivates them?" Of course they are trying to provide for themselves and their families. It has become a full-time job just to put food on the table and pay the mortgage.

But one must also wonder how they stay so motivated, what they must feel when that alarm clock blares at 5:00 a.m. after just five hours of sleep, what gets them moving in the morning? For, you see, they know what we all know. Although they truly love this country, they know their government has failed them. They give Congress approval ratings in the low teens, not because of a stereotypical distrust of politicians, but because they know their elected representatives are taking money from special interests to vote against the common interest of the people and the public good. They work for very big corporations, but many don't like it. They know these corporations care only about their profits and that concern for employees extends only to the point where it might impact profitability. They watch as their corporate employers do everything in their power to minimize their wages, break their unions, cut their benefits, rob their pensions, and shift as much business risk as they can from the corporation balance sheet onto their backs.

We are getting dangerously close to the day when these hard-working Americans refuse to answer the bell of their morning alarm clocks. The day is not far off when many will just roll over, adjust the pillow, and say, "It's just not worth it."

Depending on whose numbers you believe, this may already be happening. The Bush administration would like you to believe that unemployment in this country is only 4.8 percent. Of course, this only counts those people who are actively looking for a new job, who religiously report to the unemployment office to fill out forms and pick up unemployment checks. The percentage reported as unemployed does not include those people who have exhausted their unemployment insurance, those people who are not report-ing to the government that they are unemployed, those people who are not as active in seeking employment as the government man-dates, those people who are partially employed because they cannot find full-time jobs, those people who quit looking because they are discouraged in their job search, many of the elderly who stand no chance of finding a job given the hiring bias against them, and, of course, illegal aliens, deadbeat dads, ex-inmates violating parole, and others who are not working, but for varied reasons do not wish to inform the government of their whereabouts. There is a real unemployment figure that tries better to capture the total number of underemployed, and it currently stands closer to 12 percent.[2] If everyone were included, including those that are purposely avoid-ing detection, most assuredly the number would be north of 18 percent. This can be seen in the total employment figures for the country, which are more accurate and easier to measure than unemployment figures. In the first quarter of 2008, there were 146 million Americans reported as working out of a total of 243 million Americans of working age.[3] Even after making allowances for full-time housewives and the elderly, these figures suggest that the 18 percent figure may be conservative.

Another warning sign that all is not right in middle America is the number of adult married men who are not working. Over the last four decades, this number has consistently increased from approximately 10 to 22 percent.[4] True, the number of married women that are working has increased during this period from 32 to 62 percent,[5] so one explanation may be that married men are retiring and letting their wives bring home a paycheck. But another possible explanation is that more and more men are failing to answer the alarm.

Obama has spoken frequently about the greatness of the American dream, saying that each of us has the opportunity to be whatever we want to be and to do whatever we want to do. On November 7, 2007 he addressed a crowd in Bettendorf, Iowa before the Iowa primary and spoke on reclaiming the American Dream:

> This is what we must do to reclaim the American dream. We know it won't be easy. We'll hear from the can't-do, won't-do, won't-even-try crowd in Washington; the special interests and their lobbyists; the conventional thinking that says this country is just too divided to make progress.
>
> Well I'm not running for President to conform to this conventional thinking I'm running to challenge it. There is too much at stake. Too much at stake for the family that can't get ahead; the elderly worker who faces a retirement filled with worry; the kid who doesn't believe America has a place for her dreams. . . .
>
> It's change that I've been fighting for since I moved out to Chicago over two decades ago. Because those dreams— American dreams—are worth fighting for. And because I wouldn't be standing on this stage today if it weren't for the dreams of those who came before me . . .

America is the sum of our dreams. And what binds us together, what makes us one American family, is that we stand up and fight for each other's dreams. . . . It's time to do that once more. It's time to reclaim the American dream.[6]

As a constitutional scholar, Obama realizes that this ideal of opportunity for all is incorporated in our founding fathers words, an individual right to life, liberty and the pursuit of happiness. The pursuit of happiness. Opportunity. This is what made America different from its European forefathers. Many European countries, at one time or another, were monarchies. The key to understanding the futility of living in a monarchy is not just the great disparity of wealth and privilege. It is that one's right to such wealth is established at birth, not by your character, your efforts, and your intellect, but rather by your blood. The offense is not just that there are classes of rich and poor, but that it is impossible for an individual to move between the two. Such a bold restriction on economic opportunity constrains economic growth, because those with title do not have to work to keep it, and those without royal blood can work hard their whole lives and never attain it. In this system, there is no hope of your children advancing further than yourself.

Obama has done a great deal of thinking about the root causes of the vast inequality we see. A person who grew up poor in inferior schools cannot do well in his job interview because he has difficulty presenting his thoughts verbally and in writing. Tracing backward down the timeline, we find that low and moderate income people, on average, do worse throughout their school years than those from higher-income families. If we follow the timeline trajectory further backwards, we see that by the time they arrive at first grade, low-income children are at a tremendous disadvantage compared to their richer classmates. Traveling further back, we see that the poor are less likely to have formal preschool education, and that their parents often don't motivate them to read and to learn. But Obama wanted to know where this pattern actually starts.

He concluded it starts at birth. Regardless of the well-known and highly touted exceptions, the general rule in this country is that if you are born into poverty your fate is pretty much sealed. Imagine, for a moment, the difference between the life of someone born black in the inner city of Chicago to a poor single mother working two jobs, and someone born white in Seattle as the son of a person like Bill Gates. There is nothing equal about the opportunity for these two newborns. In fact, Obama cites that because of inherited wealth and the opportunities it provides, the wealthier newborn will see, on average, more parental reading as a baby, more books around the home, more preschool, better elementary schools, the best private prep schools, the top universities, and business opportunities in our finest corporations that the poorer newborn can only dream about.

Obama's plan to improve economic opportunity for all is fourfold. He wants to maintain an inheritance tax on our wealthiest citizens that others have fought to end, he wishes to introduce universal preschool education to give poorer children the same opportunities at early learning as their richer classmates, he wants to improve our public education system and encourage college education for all, and he wants to make sure that all artificial barriers to personal advancement are eliminated in the workplace. Let us examine each of his proposals in more detail.

Obama has realized that it is impossible to talk about equal opportunity if a society bases all privilege and opportunity primarily on the wealth of one's parents.[7] There is very little difference between a system that allows perpetual inheritance of accumulated family wealth and the opportunities that brings, and the European monarchies that America supposedly outgrew at its founding. If the greatest predictor of one's success in life is how much money they inherited from their parents, then the country quickly becomes one of permanent class distinctions, in which the probability of a poor person making good today is no better than a peasant in the Middle Ages growing up to be king. Not that it can't happen, but the odds are certainly against it.

This is what is most disturbing about the current debate about inheritance taxes in America. Regardless of how the debate turns out, much of the talk is about the unfairness of paying taxes at death, or the unfairness of paying taxes twice, or how unfair the tax is to small family business owners and small farmers who only have $10 million of property to give to their children. It is doubly disconcerting that this is the limit of the debate, because such arguments favor only the wealthy elite, a group to which most newspaper, television, and radio owners who employ those who are doing the reporting already belong. Our media is not structured to allow for a healthy debate on issues involving the rich and poor because the poor never own media outlets.

What Obama finds most disturbing about the inheritance tax debate is that the most important implication of allowing large inheritances is that it will indeed create a society based on inherited wealth privilege and opportunity. He believes that we will again become what we broke away from, an indentured people to a privileged class. Class and success based on blood, not meritocracy. Three lone voices in the wilderness appreciate how important it is to not allow economic opportunity to be inherited with one's eye color: Warren Buffett, William Henry Gates, Sr., and Barack Obama.

What is ridiculous about the debate is that we already have exemptions for inheritances up to approximately $2 million, so no one can cite a single example of a small businessman or small farmer losing his assets because of inheritance taxes. Many of the wealthy employ sophisticated annuity, charity and gifting schemes to avoid the inheritance tax entirely. There are only a very few extremely wealthy individuals who end up paying the inheritance tax at all. In effect, because capital gains taxes are forgiven on an estate, all that happens is that a higher tax rate is applied to a person's long-term capital gains due to the inheritance tax. Obama quotes Buffet in his book, *The Audacity of Hope*. "When you get rid of the estate tax," Buffett said, "you're basically handing over command of the country's resources to people who didn't earn it. It's like choosing the 2020 Olympic team by picking the children of all the winners at the 2000 games."[8]

Preserving the inheritance tax is not going to make a level playing field for all children born in America. Another of Obama's initiatives is to direct more resources to our poorer rural and inner-city neighborhoods to improve the communities and give the young children a fighting chance. Obama would like to see all young parents attend classes on childrearing so they can do a better job raising their families. He is in favor of housing development projects that allow for a range of incomes, so as not to create ghetto conditions where only the very poor live. And he believes jobs for the poor will be instrumental in holding families together and providing the parenting every young child needs.

Obama has too many initiatives to strengthen the family and provide a better learning environment for the young child to describe them all in detail here. A partial listing would include:

PROVIDE A LIVING WAGE: Barack Obama believes that people who work full-time should not live in poverty. Before the Democrats took back Congress, the minimum wage had not changed in ten years. Even though the minimum wage will rise to $7.25 an hour by 2009, the minimum wage's real purchasing power will still be below what it was in 1968. As president, Obama would further raise the minimum wage, index it to inflation and increase the Earned Income Tax Credit to make sure that full-time workers can earn a living wage that allows them to raise their families and pay for basic needs such as food, transportation, and housing—things so many people take for granted.

EXPAND THE EARNED INCOME TAX CREDIT: Under the Obama plan, full-time workers making minimum wage would get an EITC benefit up to $555, more than three times greater than the

$175 benefit they get today. If the workers are responsibly supporting their children on child support, the Obama plan would give those workers a benefit of $1,110.

EXPAND PAID SICK DAYS: Half of all private sector workers have no paid sick days and the problem is worse for employees in low-paying jobs, where less than a quarter receive any paid sick days. Barack Obama will require that employers provide seven paid sick days per year.

EXPAND THE FAMILY AND MEDICAL LEAVE ACT (FMLA): Barack Obama will expand the FMLA to cover businesses with twenty-five or more employees. Barack Obama will expand the FMLA to cover more purposes as well, including allowing workers to take leave for elder care needs; allowing parents up to twenty-four hours of leave each year to participate in their children's academic activities at school; allowing leave to be taken for purposes of caring for individuals who reside in their home for six months or more; and expanding FMLA to cover leave for employees to address domestic violence and sexual assault.

ENCOURAGE STATES TO ADOPT PAID LEAVE: As president, Barack Obama will initiate a fifty-state strategy to encourage all of the states to adopt paid-leave systems.

EXPAND HIGH-QUALITY AFTERSCHOOL OPPORTUNITIES: Barack Obama will double funding for the main federal support for afterschool programs, the twenty-first Century Learning Centers program, to serve one million more children.

EXPAND THE CHILD AND DEPENDENT CARE TAX CREDIT: Barack Obama will reform the Child and Dependent Care Tax Credit by making it refundable and allowing low-income families to receive up to a 50 percent credit for their child care expenses.[9]

Obama believes education is the key to all opportunity. People naturally assume that private schools do a much better job of educating their students than public schools; that is why parents are willing to pay $10,000 to $25,000 per year to enroll their children in private schools. The entire concept of private schools seems to violate the principle of equal opportunity for all of our children. But a recent study shows that after adjusting for the different backgrounds of the students in public and private schools, the public schools perform almost as well as private schools on standardized testing. In other words, allowing for differences in family incomes and the education level of the parents, there is very little discernible difference in testing scores between public school students and private school students.

Even if the schools offer similar curriculums and the teachers turn out to be just as good in the public schools, the very fact that the parents who are most concerned about their children's education would exit the public school system in favor of private schools puts a tremendous bias on the comparative performance of the two systems. Imagine a teacher at a private school facing thirty concerned parents at each parent teacher conference, versus a public school teacher who might have to beg three or four to attend at all. In essence, by allowing a separate, private school system, we have taken our most concerned and involved parents out of the public system entirely. You can be sure that if all private schools were closed, and the children currently in private schools were forced to attend public schools, their parents, given their emphasis on quality education, would very quickly fix whatever is currently wrong with our public schools. Don't worry, these thoughts are only mine, and do not reflect any stated position of Obama.

Not that there aren't plenty of low-performing public schools whose problems need addressing. Obama realizes that a great majority of these poorly performing public schools are in poorer neighborhoods. It is probably true, given that schools are funded with local property taxes primarily, that the schools suffer from a funding disadvantage relative to those public schools in the richer suburbs. They don't have as much money to attract quality teachers, and pay for textbooks and teaching aids. But it is not all about the money. Many of the students in the poor neighborhoods come to school less motivated to learn and less prepared to read and write.

Obama has a detailed plan for early childhood education.[10] His "zero to five" plan will provide critical support to young children and their parents. Unlike other plans, Obama's places key emphasis on early care and education, which is essential to prepare children to enter kindergarten. Obama would like to see states move toward voluntary, universal preschool. Obama would also quadruple funding for early head start and increase head start funding to improve the quality of both. Finally, he wants to see renewed emphasis on developing high quality child care programs when both parents are at work.

Obama also has detailed plans to improve our nation's primary and secondary schools. Again, it is best to quote directly from the extensive list of initiatives Obama proposes in his policy briefs on education:

REFORM NO CHILD LEFT BEHIND: Obama will reform No Child Left Behind, which starts by funding the law. Obama believes teachers should not be forced to spend the academic year preparing students to fill in bubbles on standardized tests.

MAKE MATH AND SCIENCE EDUCATION A NATIONAL PRIORITY: Obama will recruit math and science degree graduates to the teaching profession and will support efforts to help these teachers learn from professionals in the field.

ADDRESS THE DROPOUT CRISIS: Obama will address the dropout crisis by passing his legislation to provide funding to school districts to invest in intervention strategies in middle school—strategies such as personal academic plans, teaching teams, parent involvement, mentoring, intensive reading and math instruction, and extended learning time.

EXPAND HIGH-QUALITY AFTERSCHOOL OPPORTUNITIES: Obama will double funding for the main federal support for afterschool programs, the twenty-first Century Learning Centers program, to serve one million more children.

RECRUIT, PREPARE, RETAIN, AND REWARD AMERICA'S TEACHERS: Obama will create new Teacher Service Scholarships that will cover four years of undergraduate or two years of graduate teacher education. To help retain our teachers, Obama's plan will expand mentoring programs that pair experienced teachers with new recruits. Obama will promote new and innovative ways to increase teacher pay that are developed with teachers, not imposed on them.[11]

Assuming the student manages to survive elementary and secondary school, Obama wants to make college more affordable and accessible to all.[12] He has proposed creating a new American Opportunity Tax Credit. This universal credit will ensure that the first $4,000 of a college education is completely free for most Americans, cover two thirds of the cost of tuition at the average public university, and make community college completely free for most students. This is a reversal of President Reagan's policy of allowing universities to charge whatever they like, causing students and their parents to go into great debt to pay the tuition bill.

Not only will Obama's plan make college accessible to all, but it will prevent the current situation in which students graduate with high ideals, but with crippling debt on their shoulders. Many students come out of graduate programs at our best universities with student loans totaling more than $200,000. In addition to this, credit card companies on their campuses have been glad to give students an additional $5,000 to $10,000 of credit, which needs to be repaid by the student. Finally, if the student wants to enter the workforce and settle down, he will very quickly find that a home purchase requires an additional multi-hundred thousand dollar mortgage. The sad thing is not just that the young person is in debt. The truly sad part of this is that before he has had a chance to get out into the world, explore, and make his own decisions as to what his life calling might be, he feels compelled to settle into a corporate job in a small cubicle with an income sufficient to pay his debts back. He might have thought he wanted to be a teacher, an author or an artist, but necessity tells him he will be an accountant, a bank teller, or a corporate bureaucrat pushing papers for the rest of his life. We spend twenty years educating our children to widen their horizons, and then, before they can demonstrate their genius, we force them to narrow them.

Once a student graduates, he or she will have to face the very real world of business, which has its own economic opportunity issues to deal with. The business world has come a long way in the last fifty years as far as offering real economic opportunity to individuals. There was a time, not so long ago, where if you were black, or a woman, or Hispanic, or overweight, or had a disability you had no chance at getting past the interview stage of a large corporation's hiring process. And even if you did, there was a glass ceiling preventing you from ever achieving your goals and entering executive management ranks. Today, that is no longer true. If you are black and you've graduated from Harvard, summa cum laude, you will have offers from corporations around the world that would love to have you come join them. But if you are black or white, and walk in off the street after serving a couple of years in prison for a drug offense, and just need some help getting started again, you will face a much more difficult time. Don't kid yourself. There is still an enormous amount of prejudice in the workforce.

In his speech on race in America entitled, "A More Perfect Union,"[13] Obama said, "A lack of economic opportunity among black men, and the shame and frustration that came from not being able to provide for one's family, contributed to the erosion of black families, a problem that welfare policies for many years may have worsened."

In the same speech, Obama explained that you cannot understand a black person's perspective on opportunity without understanding the black man's history in the United States:

> Segregated schools were, and are, inferior schools; we still haven't fixed them, fifty years after Brown versus Board of Education, and the inferior education they provided, then and now, helps explain the pervasive achievement gap between today's black and white students. Legalized discrimination—where blacks were prevented, often through violence, from owning property, or loans were not granted to African-American business owners, or black homeowners could not access FHA mortgages, or blacks were excluded from unions, or the police force, or fire departments—meant that black families could not amass any meaningful wealth to bequeath to future generations. That history helps explain the wealth and income gap between black and white, and the concentrated pockets of poverty that persists in so many of today's urban and rural communities.[14]

In the speech in Philadelphia, Obama stated what no one else had voiced—but no one disagreed with, either:

> Two hundred and twenty-one years ago, in a hall that still stands across the street, a group of men gathered and, with these simple words, launched America's improbable experiment in democracy . . .
>
> The document they produced was eventually signed but ultimately unfinished. It was stained by this nation's orig-

inal sin of slavery, a question that divided the colonies and brought the convention to a stalemate until the founders chose to allow the slave trade to continue for at least twenty more years, and to leave any final resolution to future generations.

Of course, the answer to the slavery question was already embedded within our Constitution, a Constitution that had at is very core the ideal of equal citizenship under the law; a Constitution that promised its people liberty, and justice, and a union that could be and should be perfected over time.[15]

There is no question that Obama will open economic opportunity to black Americans during his administration. But he will also do whatever he can to eliminate the glass ceiling in corporations that only allows women to advance so far in the executive ranks; he will reform immigration laws so that Hispanics here are treated fairly and equally when seeking work; and he will seek to end all discrimination against Asians, Native Americans, people with disabilities, and homosexuals. Obama understands how devastating discrimination is, not only to this generation, but to all future generations.

But for all those who scratched and clawed their way to get a piece of the American Dream, there were many who didn't make it—those who were ultimately defeated, in one way or another, by discrimination. That legacy of defeat was passed on to future generations—to those young men and increasingly young women whom we see standing on street corners or languishing in our prisons, without hope or prospects for the future.[16]

Some of the concrete proposals Obama has made to ensure that all Americans are given an equal opportunity to succeed in their business and professional lives include strengthening civil rights

enforcement and combating employment discrimination by working to overturn the Supreme Court's recent ruling that curtails
racial minorities' and women's ability to challenge pay discrimination.[17] Obama will also pass the Fair Pay Act to ensure that women
receive equal pay for equal work. Obama will strengthen federal
hate crimes legislation and reinvigorate enforcement at the Department of Justice's Criminal Section. Obama will ban racial profiling
by federal law enforcement agencies, and provide federal incentives
to state and local police departments to prohibit the practice.

Today, the countries of the world are starkly divided between those
120 or so that are prosperous enough to provide a decent standard
of living for the majority of their citizens, and those fifty or so
countries, some with great natural resource wealth, whose citizenry
is scratching by on less than two dollars a day in income. There is
a distinct and fundamental difference between these rich and poor
countries.[18] The richer countries are better educated, respect individual rights, and have liberal democratic governments and
capitalist economic systems. The poor countries are much less well
educated, exhibit permanent class differences, are ruled by mon-
archs or dictators, and have fewer civil liberties, less press freedom
and stunted economies. Whatever free markets they may espouse
are tightly constrained by government regulation and dominated
by monopolies controlled by friends of the ruling party.[19] The average citizen is unlikely to be highly motivated to work hard and seek
advancement in such a rigged system. There are very good reasons
why societies based on permanent class differences are not very
efficient, economically speaking. As Obama has said, it is important in any economy that all participants be highly motivated to
work hard to improve their own lot and the welfare of others.
Whether it be the feudal peasant, the poor tribal African, or the
hard-working American on his way to work at 6:00 a.m., it is
vitally important to the functioning of a healthy economy to keep
everyone highly motivated.

A second advantage of such a bottom-up economic system is that it allows genius to percolate up from anywhere in the population. If you believe that genius is fairly randomly distributed in a population, then it would be hurtful to the very fabric of society to disenfranchise 95 percent of the people by denying them educational opportunity. Is it more likely that the next Warren Buffett or Bill Gates will come from a country that opens its educational and business opportunities to all, or from a country that opens its best schools and prime positions only to the ruling elite? You would have to be quite the elitist to believe that a system that limits opportunity only to the privileged has the best chance of finding the truly unique individual who will create the breakthrough invention or business leading to tremendous economic benefits for all.

Another huge advantage of bottom-up economics quickly became apparent to me when I traveled to Jordan in 2003 to advise the kingdom on how it might best stimulate economic growth. As I traveled around the kingdom, I was struck by the fact that many Jordanians were much less busy than their king. Daily, the Jordanian newspapers reported that the king was meeting with Microsoft about providing—there's that word again—one hundred jobs in the capital, or the king was discussing a possible purchase of telecommunications equipment to provide telephones to his citizens with AT&T. It appeared that many Jordanians were quite satisfied waiting for their king to provide them jobs, instead of going out and creating job opportunities themselves. It was a job for many Jordanians just to keep up in the newspapers with the daily exploits of the King. This is a prime example of a top-down economy. No matter how busy and well-intentioned the king was, no matter how many business meetings he held each day, he could not stimulate economic growth even a fraction as much as millions of ordinary Jordanians could were they to begin making their own business deals and arranging their own business meetings.[20]

Obama understands the power of a bottom-up economy as well as anybody.[21] He is not just contrasting it to the failed trickle-down economic policies of the Bush administration. Obama's under-standing of the power of a bottom-up economy isn't just about who is favored by the government's tax cut policies. He understands that for a healthy economy to prosper and grow, it needs the involve-ment of all of its citizens. His background as a constitutional scholar and his work community organizing in Chicago with aver-age Americans who had little hope for a better future have helped him understand the importance of creating opportunity for all.

Chapter Three

THE CURRENT FINANCIAL CRISIS

It's useful to remind ourselves, then, that our free market system is the result neither of natural law nor of Divine Providence. Rather, it emerged through a painful process of trial and error, a series of difficult choices between efficiency and fairness, stability and change. And although the benefits of our free market system are mostly derived from the individual efforts of generations of men and women pursuing their own vision of happiness, in each and every period of great economic upheaval and transition we depended on government action to open up opportunity, encourage competition, and make the market work better . . . and we can be guided throughout by Lincoln's simple maxim: that we will do collectively, through our government, only those things that we cannot do as well, or at all, individually and privately.[1]

With these words Obama has told you his overall economic philosophy. He understands the power of the free market to create jobs and encourage creativity, but he also understands that, left to its own devices, without proper government oversight, it has a way of bouncing wildly between booms and busts. Individual participants in a market economy can do little to influence the overall stability of the system, but government can, and must, act to assure our financial markets remain strong and stable.

Circle one. A) The United States economy is healthy and vibrant, but suffering a minor downturn. B) the United States is in recession and experiencing negative growth, but it will be short lived. C) the United States is in a severe recession, which threatens causing a global downturn. D) the United States is facing the most serious threat to its financial system and to its economy since 1929.

The way you answer this question will determine how appropriate you believe government action is in spurring our economy and coming to the aid of our financial system. It is impossible to put Obama's economic plan into perspective without first reviewing how serious the current crisis is. Let us take the first half of this chapter to review how we got into this mess, and then analyze Obama's plan to get us out. It may be more background information than you would like, but if you are a homeowner or a concerned citizen worried about your country's financial system, it will be time well spent. You will conclude, 1) the problem is much bigger than it is being made out to be, and final losses will be in the multiple trillions of dollars worldwide, 2) we are not yet halfway into the national housing price decline, 3) this crisis did not happen by accident, but was a direct result of the lack of regulation in the finance industry that occurs when Wall Street is the biggest dollar contributor to your elected representatives' campaigns, and 4) it will take all the wisdom of our President and our Congress to extricate us from this financial disaster without causing a lengthy worldwide recession.

In 2005 an ambitious young associate at a major New York investment banking firm made an error while feeding data to the firm's credit risk analyzing program. The program was designed to predict, based on macroeconomic data, which developing countries from the Third World were at the greatest risk of defaulting on their debts. Rather than inputting economic data on just the developing countries, this young associate mistakenly input data on all the countries of the world, including the most advanced countries of the world. To his his firms' surprise, the system spit out red warning flags highlighting the United States as a country with significant risk of bankruptcy. Not knowing that the United States was not a developing country, the computer program evaluated its $10 trillion of debt relative as a percentage of its GDP of 72 percent, its large government operating deficit of $350 billion, and its annual trade deficit, which had leapt from $100 billion to over $700 billion in the last ten years, and concluded that the United States faced significant risk of defaulting on its Treasury obligations.

This is important background information, as it paints a much larger canvas of economic problems for the United States than simply a housing price decline. Of course, the housing price decline nationally was the trigger and the major cause of the current financial crisis. Initially described as a subprime problem limited to approximately $1.3 trillion of subprime mortgages extended to borrowers with weak credit histories, it rapidly expanded to include $500 billion of prime mortgages that were known as NINJA loans. NINJA stood for no income, no job, no application, and was shorthand for loans that were extended with no income verification process, such that the borrower or the mortgage broker could fabricate qualifying income at will. It did not stop there. Fairly quickly much of the $4 trillion of CDOs, collateralized debt obligations, outstanding, many of them rated AAA, were found to be in serious risk of default. CDOs were a Wall Street invention, and are nothing more than a layered packaging or pooling of individual mortgages that allow their sale to pension funds, municipalities and foreign governments.

Then it was determined that there was $1.5 trillion of adjustable-rate mortgages that were due to reset to a much higher mortgage payment in 2008 and 2009. The backstop provided by monoline mortgage insurance companies turned out to be worth not much more than the paper their guarantees were written on, as the small highly leveraged monoline insurance companies in the end had guaranteed hundreds of times their total capital in mortgage securities. Fannie Mae and Freddie Mac, government-sponsored entities that were supposed to provide stability to the mortgage markets, turned out to have credit losses themselves in their $5.2 trillion loan and guarantee portfolio. They were in no position to stabilize the market as they went into the crisis leveraged more than a hundred to one with debt to equity.[2]

If anyone thinks that the current financial crisis is going to end quickly, they need to review the magnitude of the assets that are in trouble. The market value of all residential homes in the United States in 2006 was $24 trillion. That is $24 trillion with a T. In other words, $24,000 billion, or 24 million bags of one million dollars each. Total mortgage debt on these properties exceeded $12 trillion. For comparison purposes, the total market value of all publicly traded companies in the United States in 2006 was $15 trillion. If real estate prices declined by some 30 percent nationally, about what I anticipate in real terms, this would represent a $7.2 trillion loss of wealth, approximately equal to half the value of all the common stocks in America and more than half of the entire GDP of the United States. It is important to note that while many suggest that the world economy will prevent the United States from entering a severe recession, India's economy is only $1.7 trillion in size and China's stands at $3 trillion (actual exchange rates, not PPP). Not only are these economies too small to save the United States, but to a great degree their economies depend on exports to the United States as their primary engine, and so will end up suffering right along with us.

I have been predicting a real estate collapse since 2003, the date my first book on the subject was published.[3] In early 2006, I published my second book[4] on the housing mess and predicted national real estate declines of approximately 25 to 30 percent and worst-case scenarios in certain California and Florida cities of 40 to 50 percent. At the time, given that the residential real estate market had increased in value every single year for fifty straight years, many dismissed these forecasts as wildly overly pessimistic. Now, only eighteen months into an expected five to seven year real estate downturn, home prices have already declined 15 percent in real terms nationally. Certain cities such as Miami, San Francisco and Las Vegas have seen real price declines of 25 percent or more. The question everyone is asking is, is it over? Unfortunately, no.

As housing prices decline, more and more Americans owe more on their mortgage than their house is worth. Under such circumstances, many Americans have come to the conclusion that it makes more sense to turn the house keys over to the bank than continue to make mortgage payments. The number of foreclosures is spiking, first on those homes that were purchased in the high home price environment of 2006 and 2007. Those purchased in 2005, 2004, and so on will default until prices reach a more normal level. It should scare you that a majority of the damage done to date has been done primarily only by 2006 and 2007 mortgages defaulting. If prices return to more normal 1997 levels, there will be an enormous number of Americans who face default and foreclosure on their home mortgages. Some have estimated that as many as 10 million Americans may lose their homes.

The reason that one can be fairly certain that prices will continue to fall is because prices never should have gotten to these levels to begin with. Prices across the country went from a typical two-and-a-half times household income to a much more aggressive four to five times household income. In some cities like San Diego, the average home was selling at eleven times the average household income at the market peak. The primary reason for such high prices paid was loose credit. The banks, for whatever reason, were willing to lend astronomical sums of money to potential homebuyers. The two fundamental errors the banks made were 1) they did not understand that defaults would explode if prices ever began to come down, and, 2) their lending formula had a fundamental error in it. Looking back, common sense dictates that in a rising market, even a homeowner in trouble would rather sell his home and net a small equity profit than default to the bank. This of course changes in a declining price market, where the home is underwater. The homeowner has no motivation to sell and face a loss, so he puts the asset back to the bank by defaulting, and the foreclosure rate explodes in a down house price environment.

There is also a fundamental problem in the way most banks determine the amount of money that they will lend to potential homebuyers. Banks do the calculation based solely on a couple's earning power in the first year, totally ignoring the impact of general inflation in the future on the household's earnings power and the value of the collateral, the home. During periods of high inflation, like the 1970s, the bank's simple, but wrong, qualifying formula tells the bank to underlend, and home prices are constrained. During periods of low inflation, like the last ten years, the bank's qualifying formula suggests the bank overextend, and home prices accelerate to a point beyond any ability of a homeowner to repay loans. The key to understanding this phenomenon is to realize that although mortgage interest rates have declined from 15 percent in the 1970s to 4.5 percent in 2006, the real rate of interest did not change materially. It is, and always has been, approximately 2.5 to 3 percent per year. If real interest rates didn't change, home prices should not have changed materially over the decade.[5]

What this means is that now banks have recognized where they are. They understand that foreclosures explode in a declining price market, and hopefully some of them have begun to understand that their qualifying formula needs some adjustment to account for general inflation in the economy. Homeowners have also adjusted. Where they had mistakenly thought in the past that a home was a great investment that can only increase in value, they now understand that like all investments, homes can go down in value. This is extremely relevant, because once you realize that homes can go down in value, you are much less likely to buy second homes, vacation homes, investment properties, or to overextend yourself and invest millions in your primary residence. It turns out that if you are living in the home, it isn't an investment at all, it is pure consumption, because rather than owning the home and putting rental income in the bank like an investment, you are forgoing all rental income by living on the property.

Assuming banks have woken up to the error in their ways, they will probably no longer be offering mortgages at ten to twelve times a household income. Simple math dictates that if they pull back and start writing mortgages at a more reasonable five to six times homebuyer's income, housing prices will have to adjust downward by some 40 to 50 percent to make up for this difference in financing—that is, unless the homebuyer wishes to write a much larger down payment on the home, something homebuyers have shown no desire of doing to date.

The bottom line is that we can expect real home prices to decline further, some 25 to 30 percent nationally, and 40 to 50 percent on the coasts and in Las Vegas and Phoenix. Everything to date has been prologue. The early foreclosures were primarily speculators in non-owner occupied investment properties, some second homes, and vacation homes. Foreclosures going forward now will be felt to a much greater degree by homeowners living in their primary residences. The most leveraged buyers were hit first, but now even more conservative buyers, who put down 20 percent deposits on their homes, will see their savings, their deposits and their homes evaporate.[6]

Is this a housing collapse, or a liquidity crunch, or a meltdown of our entire financial system? While the decline in home prices occurred first, it is not the average homeowner who is suffering. As a matter of fact, on average, the typical homebuyer did quite well during this period. Imagine a homeowner whose house appreciated from $250,000 to $500,000 and decided to sell. He has $250,000 in the bank he wouldn't otherwise have had. Now assume he borrows $1 million from a bank to buy a $1 million home with no money down. He lives the life of luxury for one to two years, pays very little interest on an adjustable rate mortgage with an initial teaser rate, and then goes six to nine months more, paying no interest, until the bank forecloses and he must leave his million dollar home. Assume all the home prices in his neighborhood now readjust back to the prices they were at before the recent housing boom. He borrows $250,000 from his bank, buys his old house for $250,000, and still has $250,000 cash in the bank. Somehow, in this loopy circuitous market, he comes out $250,000 ahead. Very similar arithmetic can show that someone who didn't move, but refinanced his home for $1 million at the peak and used the money to buy cars, boats and to pay off other personal debt, like student loans or credit card debt, is also much better off if he defaults to the bank on his million dollar mortgage and returns to a more modestly priced home.

Of course, the losers in this loop are the lenders. They loaned $1 million on a home that turned out to be worth $500,000 which they now own on their books and are trying to sell in a down real estate market. They have very real losses of a half-million dollars. Although one cannot generalize across all circumstances, this simple example shows that it is the banks and the lenders that are the losers in this high leverage dance. And the winners are those homeowners who sold their homes or refinanced them at the peak of the market and then defaulted on the underlying mortgage as housing prices declined. I am not trying to assign blame to either party, although there is a lot of that to go around, only to show that it is the banks that are the big financial losers here.

The irony is that even though it was the drastic home price contraction that set off this crisis, the real losers are not on Main Street, but on Wall Street. Commercial banks, investment banks and their investing clients worldwide that hold these overpriced mortgages are the real losers. It also tells you that if you wish to assist the market in overcoming this crisis, the majority of your effort should be directed at the financial system, not homeowners, regardless of how unpopular that may be politically.

Of course, all we have talked about so far is the problem in aggregate. One must look beyond simple averages to see the real human suffering of this crisis. While it is true that the commercial banks and mortgage investment community are the big dollar losers in terms of dollars in this fiasco, there is a human component of people who have been greatly wronged and harmed.

Homebuyers of more modest means were clearly pushed into purchasing homes that they could not afford by an aggressive cabal of real estate agents, appraisers, greedy mortgage brokers, and fraudulent predatory lenders. The rule of these middlemen agents was to close the deal regardless of the pain involved for the homebuyer. They were indifferent as to what price was paid by the homeowner, so long as the deal closed and they got paid their fees.

We have seen that the lenders themselves were mostly indifferent to how high prices got, because typically they did not hold the mortgage asset, but sold it upstream to other investors. But predatory lenders also benefited if they held the mortgage paper, as they often overloaded the homebuyers with unmanageable debt, then grabbed their houses from them and resold them in an escalating market.

Here are just a few of the concrete proposals Obama has made to address predatory lending and fraudulent activity in the mortgage and credit card businesses. I quote:

PROTECT HOMEOWNERSHIP AND CRACK DOWN ON MORTGAGE FRAUD: Obama will crack down on fraudulent brokers and lenders. He will also make sure homebuyers have honest and complete information about their mortgage options, and he will give a tax credit to all middle-class homeowners.

ENSURE MORE ACCOUNTABILITY IN THE SUBPRIME MORTGAGE INDUSTRY: Obama has been closely monitoring the subprime mortgage situation for years, and introduced comprehensive legislation over a year ago to fight mortgage fraud and protect consumers against abusive lending practices. Obama's STOP FRAUD Act provides the first federal definition of mortgage fraud, increases funding for federal and state law enforcement programs, creates new criminal penalties for mortgage professionals found guilty of fraud, and requires industry insiders to report suspicious activity.

MANDATE ACCURATE LOAN DISCLOSURE: Obama will create a Homeowner Obligation Made Explicit (HOME) score, which will provide potential borrowers with a simplified, standardized borrower metric (similar to APR) for home mortgages. The HOME score will allow individuals to easily compare various mortgage products and understand the full cost of the loan.

CLOSE BANKRUPTCY LOOPHOLE FOR MORTGAGE COMPANIES: Obama will work to eliminate the provision that prevents bankruptcy courts from modifying an individual's mortgage payments. Obama believes that the subprime mortgage industry, which has engaged in dangerous and sometimes unscrupulous business practices, should not be shielded by outdated federal law.

ADDRESS PREDATORY CREDIT CARD PRACTICES: Obama will establish a five-star rating system so that every consumer knows the risk involved in every credit card. He also will establish a Credit Card Bill of Rights to stop credit card companies from exploiting consumers with unfair practices . . . The Obama plan will ban unilateral charges, apply interest rate increases only to future debt, prohibit interest on fees, prohibit "universal defaults," require prompt and fair crediting of cardholder payments, reform bankruptcy laws.

CAP OUTLANDISH INTEREST RATES ON PAYDAY LOANS AND IMPROVE DISCLOSURE: Obama supports extending a 36 percent interest cap to all Americans. Obama will require lenders to provide clear and simplified information about loan fees, payments and penalties, which is why he'll require lenders to provide this information during the application process.[7]

How effective will these suggested solutions to this crisis be? It is important to realize the sheer magnitude of this crisis, so that minor political feel-good efforts are exposed for what they are: worthless. Also, it is critical to understand that this is not primarily a home-owner problem. Many homeowners got out at the peak, grabbed value for themselves by defaulting to their bank or, if they did nothing during the decade, just saw their home price appreciate rapidly and then return to where it was previously. To be effective in addressing this problem, you have to understand it is a banking problem and an investor problem, that it is huge, measured in the multiple trillions of dollars, and that it is not about liquidity or giving the banks more cash to lend. It is about bank losses that are so large as to threaten the solvency of our largest banks and investment banks and, possibly, the entire financial system.

Finally, the entire mortgage and real estate market has turned out to be corrupt and unregulated. Realtors cared more about getting paid their fees than properly advising their clients on what price to pay or accept, appraisers were anything but independent as they shopped their valuations to get business, mortgage brokers fraudulently changed mortgage applications so that applicants had sufficient incomes reported to qualify for the necessary financing, and bankers, with the help of the corrupted rating agencies, packaged junk mortgage securities as AAA and sold them to institutional investors who never did the due diligence they should have, but rather relied on the rating of the securities they bought.

Now let us examine Obama's economic agenda, and how he intends to deal with this financial crisis.[8] As we have seen, Obama is committed to stopping predatory lending. Through his community organization work in Chicago, Obama saw the benefits to the neighborhood and to the nation of homeownership. Community organizations were instrumental in providing counseling to new homeowners in poor neighborhoods so that they would understand the commitment they were undertaking, and understand the math behind a typical residential mortgage. Unfortunately, due to a lack of regulation, an entire industry of predatory lenders grew up. They were not interested in seeing homeownership increase in our nation. There were only interested in maximizing their profits, regardless of how unscrupulous their practices. They would lie to homeowners to get them to sign mortgage notes, they would fraudulently change income data on applications to get bank approval, and they would hide exorbitant fees and high rates of interest in the details of the mortgage contracts with no explanation to the homeowner. Typically, they didn't care if there was a foreclosure or not. They had either already sold the loan upstream to another investor and pocketed their fees, or used phony default provisions to grab homes that were worth far more than their loan balances away from their owners.

In an attempt to find a scapegoat, the real estate industry, the mortgage industry and their paid shills in Washington have begun to blame the federal government for the housing crash. They claim that the CRA, the Community Reinvestment Act, which requires banks to lend money in poor neighborhoods in which they take deposits, is the real culprit.[9] They want you to believe that bad mortgage loans resulted from banks being pressured by the federal government to lend mortgage money to poor people. In a replay from the 1990s, when Newt Gingrich blamed single poor mothers for causing the government's operating deficit, now conservatives want to blame the housing crash and ensuing financial crisis on poor people, and the federal government for encouraging lending to them. In essence, they are arguing that things would have been fine with the markets except for government interference caused by too much regulation, what has become their standard litany nowadays for any problem our economy faces.

Unfortunately, the facts just don't fit. The cities that had the most rapid price appreciation of homes during the last decade and are now experiencing the biggest price declines were not homes to the poor, but rather some of the wealthiest enclaves in the country.[10] The list of cities that grew the fastest in terms of home prices, setting themselves up for the biggest declines during the collapse, reads like an episode from *Lifestyles of the Rich and Famous*; Palm Beach, Miami, San Francisco, San Diego, Palm Springs, Santa Barbara, and Beverly Hills. The only homeless person anyone ever saw in Beverly Hills was Nick Nolte in the film *Down and Out in Beverly Hills*. It turns out that price declines in percentage terms were much higher for higher priced homes than more moderately priced homes. This shows in mortgage default rates, which are lower for qualifying loans under $417,000 than for jumbo loans over that federally imposed limit. It is rare you see a poor family buying a home for more than $417,000, regardless of how much the CRA encourages home ownership for the poor.

The CRA act was passed in 1977, but homes didn't start their rapid escalation until 1997—coincidentally, just exactly when the banks, the real culprits here, started lending homebuyers eight to ten times their household incomes to buy homes, and pushing no money down, interest only, adjustable rate, and other acronym-named, crazily exotic mortgage products on the public, to help them pay even higher prices. Finally, the housing boom was not limited to the United States. Ireland, the United Kingdom, Spain, Australia, China, and India have all seen their home prices soar, and are now seeing the beginning of a global housing bust.[11] There was no Community Reinvestment Act in any of these countries.

It is important to understand this false CRA explanation for the housing market collapse. Community organizers like Obama depended on the CRA to get much needed funding to their neighborhood clients. Homes in the inner city of Chicago were being purchased by single mothers with families for $50,000 to $100,000, but these modest home prices paid were never the cause of the real estate collapse. Rather, it was the banks on the coasts that were lending thirty-year-old couples with combined incomes of $100,000 mortgage amounts exceeding $800,000 to buy the home of their dreams.

A couple can't be expected to be married forever, and of course one of them might get sick, or either might lose their job. If anything happened to change the couple's income, this highly leveraged mortgage could not be paid back in time.

But many of the poor and middle-income borrowers who did not over-borrow are indeed suffering. Obama will attempt to provide relief to them through a number of initiatives. Obama's STOP FRAUD Act provides the first federal definition of mortgage fraud, increases funding for federal and state law fraud enforcement programs, requires industry participants to report suspicious activity, and creates new criminal penalties for mortgage professionals found guilty of fraud. This bill also provides counseling to homeowners to help avoid foreclosures.[12]

As president, Obama will enact laws to ensure prospective homeowners have access to complete information about their mortgages. He will create a system that will allow individuals to easily compare various mortgage products and understand the full cost they are undertaking. In very simple language, a very short document will spell out exactly what the mortgage payments will be and tell the buyer his monthly payment commitment including any mandatory taxes and insurance.[13]

Obama has announced a $10 billion loan to assist people refinance their mortgages and avoid foreclosure. Obama recognizes that this is a very small number relative to the trillions of dollars of potential trouble of mortgages involved in the crisis. But he also realizes that it is not proper for the American taxpayer to bail out speculators, owners of second homes and vacation homes, and people living in homes much larger than they can afford. Rather than insist that homeowners be allowed to stay in large homes they never should have bought in the first place, Obama's plan will assist with relocation expenses for individuals who realize their homes are simply too expensive for their income levels, and wish to sell.[14] Obama realizes that a number of Americans gamed the system and ended up winners as a result of this housing crash, but he does not intend to reward their speculative behavior.

Obama strongly opposed the 2005 bankruptcy bill, which made it much more difficult for individuals to claim personal bankruptcy and walk away from their home mortgages. As president, Obama will seek to eliminate the federal bankruptcy laws' Chapter 13 provision that prevents bankruptcy courts from modifying principal balances and mortgage payments due under a home mortgage. Recently, the Senate said it would not be willing to allow such write downs, but we know that the Senators are receiving a great deal of their financial support from the banks who are not anxious to face up to the losses from this fiasco.[15]

The Bush administration has done very little to address this crisis. They don't want their biggest supporters, the banks and Wall Street, to own up to losses that might threaten their very solvency, and they really do believe their mantra that greater regulation of the markets is almost always bad. McCain originally said he would do nothing to help bail out homeowners or banks unless the entire financial system were threatened, a position he has been forced to reverse himself on, given the political realities of running for office.

As Obama assumes office, he will very quickly have to implement a plan of action that is bold in its vision and in its scope. A critical ingredient of his plan will have to address the undue influence that the mortgage industry, the real estate industry, the commercial banks, the investment banks, and the private equity and hedge fund industries have had in Washington through their lobbyists. Senator Charles Schumer, who sits on the banking committee (which should provide a leading role in determining Congress's plan of action in this crisis), accepted more than $3 million in campaign donations from the very industries that he is supposed to be regulating. His ten largest contributors are all commercial banks and investment banks.[16] Whose interests do you think he'll have in mind when he goes to write legislation to address this crisis? You, the American homeowner and taxpayer, or his commercial banking and investment banking buddies?

Much of the current crisis could have been avoided if not for the undue influence of lobbyists in Washington. State governments across the country have been crying out for help over the last five years, with egregious examples of predatory lending, mortgage fraud, overly aggressive bank tactics, and appraiser malfeasance. But Washington turned a deaf ear. Fannie Mae and Freddie Mac almost blew up in 2004 due to mismanagement and debt leverage of more than a hundred to one.[17] But, thanks to their contributions to their favorite senators and congressmen in both parties, by 2007, capital restrictions and lending standards on Fannie Mae and Freddie Mac were being dramatically relaxed.

Obama understands that the housing and mortgage financing crisis did not have to happen, that Washington insiders were paid to look the other way as egregious behavior was condoned, and in some cases subsidized. He gave a speech at Cooper Union in New York in March 2008,[18] in which he squarely laid the blame for the housing and financial crisis at the feet of Washington lobbyists and the elected representatives who corrupted the system by refusing to pass necessary regulation in exchange for campaign donations. It is a prime reason why he looks to unify Democrats, Independents and Republicans, as it will take a total unified effort to overcome the power exerted by corporate lobbyists in Washington.

It is reported that in 2007 financial services companies spent more than $402 million on lobbying, led by $138 million from the insurance industry. This is a record for annual giving by the financial services industry, with the exception of the $417 million they spent on lobbying in 1999 to repeal the Glass-Steagle Act. That Act had prohibited banks from getting into risky businesses, such as investment banking, that might threaten their depositors' investments. It is not coincidence that the successful repeal of the Glass-Steagle act in 1999 resulted in significant deregulation of the financial services industry, including the real estate and mortgages industry and led directly to the current crisis.[19]

Probably no other incident provides the sharp contrast of how President Obama will deal with the financial crisis as compared to the Bush administration than the decline and fall of Bear Stearns, the country's fifth largest investment bank. Like a good magician who draws your attention to his right hand waving in the air while his left hand surreptitiously picks your wallet from your pocket, the Bush administration and its Treasury Secretary, Hank Paulson, wanted you to focus on the decline of Bear Stearns, rather than the financial support they were providing their Wall Street cronies. Yes, Bear Stearns stock did indeed decline from $170 to just over $2 during a twelve-month period, before rising slightly once the government bail-out was assured. This represented an approximately $20 billion decline in value. But at the same time Hank Paulson announced Bear Stearns demise, he was magically giving J.P. Morgan $30 billion of tax-payer money to guarantee the worst mortgage assets in Bear Stearns portfolio. As if that were not enough, in the same announcement that told the world of Bear Stearn's decline and its subsequent acquisition by J.P. Morgan, the Federal Reserve announced, for the first time since 1930, that they would open the discount window to allow lending to investment banks, not just commercial banks. Finally, showing no remorse, the Federal Reserve allowed the investment banks to put up mortgage loans as collateral rather than the traditional and much less risky US Treasury bonds. Originally assumed to be a $200 billion program, it turned out there was no limit established as to how much the investment banks could borrow from the Federal Reserve.

What happened? We know that Hank Paulson was the CEO of Goldman Sachs prior to his becoming Treasury Secretary. But who benefited? J.P. Morgan shareholders, immediately upon the announcement of the Bear Stearns acquisition, saw the value of their stock holdings increase by more than $20 billion. Bear Stearns equity investors may have lost $20 billion, but their debt investors, who held more than $120 billion of Bear Stearns debt securities, were immediately made whole. They were sitting on debt securities that had been trading at $0.70 to $0.80 on the dollar, and now they were cashed out at par or given new J.P. Morgan debt worth full par value.

Who else benefited from the J.P. Morgan acquisition of Bear Stearns? Would you be surprised to learn that one of the biggest beneficiaries were the hedge funds, the hedge funds that have been one of the biggest contributors to this administration and this Congress's election campaigns? Many of these hedge funds had made bad mortgage investments themselves, and were funding their operations with Bear Stearns loans. If Bear Stearns went down, it would take them with it.

In addition, these same hedge funds are very big players in the credit derivatives market. Very small hedge funds, in a fact, write insurance policies that guarantee that firms like Bear Stearns will not default on their debt obligations. If Bear Stearns had been allowed to claim bankruptcy and default on their debt, these hedge funds would have lost an enormous amount of money. While Bear Stearns had some $120 billion of debt outstanding, there were over $2.5 trillion of credit derivatives guaranteeing that debt outstanding.

Had Bear Stearns been allowed to go on under, the hedge funds and other speculators would have lost trillions. Because Bear Stearns, with government support, was acquired by J.P. Morgan, it meant that its bonds never technically defaulted but rather were absorbed by J.P. Morgan, and became their liabilities.

One can never be sure how an Obama administration would react to a similar situation, but given that it is a hallmark of his campaign not to take lobbyists' and special interest money, one would hope he would be free to do what was right for the American taxpayer and the American homeowner. In an interview with the editorial board of the *Chicago Tribune* immediately after the announcement of the Bear Stearns bailout, he addressed the issue. The article read, "While Sen. Barack Obama said he is generally wary of government intervention to bail out struggling banks, such as the move by the Federal Reserve, Friday, aimed at preventing a collapse of Bear Stearns Co., he said exceptions can be made in an effort to prevent 'a cascading decline in credit markets.'"[20]

Obama pointed out that relaxing regulations on mortgage brokers and mortgage bundlers has effectively destroyed the credit quality of the mortgage products they were creating. These bad mortgage product investments ended up back on Wall Street, on the books of the commercial banks and investment banks, and on the balance sheets of their biggest investing clients. As Obama says, what was bad for Main Street turned out to be bad for Wall Street. In a wonderful summary of the entire episode, he said simply, "pain trickled up," and, "Our history should give us confidence that we don't have to choose between an oppressive government-run economy and a chaotic, unforgiving capitalism."

In his speech at Cooper Union in New York, Obama was the first to be brave enough to mention the "R" word, and here I am not talking about Recession.[21] The "R" word Obama emphasized was Regulation. CNBC, MSNBC, Fox news, Rush Limbaugh, Sean Hannity, and others have turned the word regulation into a dirty word. Obama understands that we cannot have free markets without regulation. It is regulation that insures that contracts in a free economy are honored. It is regulation that protects property rights and a free economy. It is regulation that allows the development of a sophisticated financial marketplace with sophisticated securities, and contracts that allow for the formation of corporations, the protection of investments, the providing of insurance, and the sharing of risk.

In his Cooper Union speech, Obama discussed regulatory changes he would recommend to better regulate Wall Street:

> Beyond dealing with the immediate housing crisis, it is time for the federal government to revamp the regulatory framework dealing with our financial markets. . . .
> First, if you can borrow from the government, you

should be subject to government oversight and supervision. . . .

Second, there needs to be general reform of the requirements to which all regulated financial institutions are subjected. Capital requirements should be strengthened, particularly for complex financial instruments like some of the mortgage securities that led to our current crisis. We must develop and rigorously manage liquidity risk. We must investigate rating agencies and potential conflicts of interest with the people they are rating. And transparency requirements must demand full disclosure by financial institutions to shareholders and counterparties. . . .

Third, we need to streamline a framework of overlapping and competing regulatory agencies. . . .

Fourth, we need to regulate institutions for what they do, not what they are. Over the last few years, commercial banks and thrift institutions were subject to guidelines on subprime mortgages that did not apply to mortgage brokers and companies. It makes no sense. . . .

Fifth, we must remain vigilant and crack down on trading activity that crosses the line to market manipulation. . . .

Sixth, we need a process that identifies systemic risks to the financial system. . . .

Finally, the American people must be able to trust that their government is looking out for all of us—not just those who donate to political campaigns.

No one is in favor of too much regulation. But this financial crisis should alert everyone to the fact that free markets cannot regulate themselves. A company's concern for its public image is not a strong enough force to overcome the company's primal instinct towards profit. There are unintended consequences of market players acting together that can never be anticipated by a single participant acting alone. As Obama says in his speech, it is completely unreasonable to expect the American taxpayer to bail out investment banks, and not expect the banks to be completely transparent and offer full disclosure to the public. As Obama summarized, ". . . the American people must be able to trust that their government is looking out for all of us, not just those who donate to political campaigns."

This speech on the importance of improving the regulation of our financial markets was one of the most brilliant I have ever witnessed. Of course it took courage to talk about increasing government regulation of anything in an election year. But it is the right answer. We know that Obama does not have the sophisticated finance background to arrive at this conclusion on his own. But, informed by his financial advisors, Obama had the wisdom to understand the problem thoroughly, and wasn't deterred by special interests or an electorate looking for easy answers. He found a solution that was not at all apparent to most everyone else. The other candidates, not to mention George W. Bush, Henry Paulson, and Ben Bernanke, were all pushing proposals that would throw taxpayer money at the failing banks, but do nothing to get at the root cause of the problem, lack of regulation. The fact that Obama was able to figure out such a complex problem in an area of finance that is not his strength speaks volumes about the effectiveness of his approach to solving problems based on honest debate and analysis, and a desire to do what is right for the American people.

Obama has already made it clear that he will come down strongly on any lending institution or mortgage company that fraudulently and purposefully tries to rip off the American consumer. One would expect Obama to tighten the licensing requirements for real estate agents and mortgage brokers, such that they have to pass financial knowledge tests similar to what a stockbroker has to do currently. After chasing the lobbyists from Washington, Obama will try to re-instill confidence in the financial system and in the government regulators that oversee them. Once Fannie Mae and Freddie Mac are prohibited from giving tens of millions of dollars in campaign donations to Congress, it might become apparent to all that they are terribly overleveraged, and would never survive as independent companies if they did not have the implied guarantee of the US taxpayer behind them.

Obama will require that the commercial banks and investment banks be properly capitalized in relation to the riskiness of their investments. He will take whatever action is necessary to re-instill confidence in the financial industry, and prevent a very serious financial crisis from turning into bank runs and a financial collapse. He will ensure that middlemen, like mortgage brokers, appraisers and real estate agents, are properly regulated, licensed and supervised. And he will come down very hard on any entity that he feels is in the business of predatory lending.

What else can Obama do to prevent crises like these from occurring again? I have some opinions that I would like to share with you, in the hopes that Obama's financial advisors may end up hearing them and then convince Obama to adopt them. I want to be clear. I believe the following proposals to have great merit, but to my knowledge, Obama has never mentioned these or similar proposals.

The housing crisis is not the first crisis our financial system has faced. Remember Mexico in 1994, Thailand in 1997, Russia's bankruptcy in 1998, the Long Term Credit Corporation bankruptcy and bail out in 1998, and the Internet stock bubble and burst in 2001. There is an enormous amount of volatility not only in our stock markets, but in our banking system. As long as the federal government stands by to bail out bankrupt investment and commercial banks, the riskiness of the system will not change. Banks achieve a higher return by taking on greater risk so long as they are protected on the downside by federal bailouts and giveaways. It is in the interest, not only of Americans, but of people everywhere, to take some of the risk, and thus some of the extreme profitability, out of the global financial system.

This can be accomplished most easily by regulating the amount of leverage in the system. The way the system works now an individual can purchase a home with no money down or 100 percent debt. This mortgage can be held by hedge funds that leverage it thirty-two to one, debt-to-equity. The hedge funds' risk exposure is actually much greater, as they also may guarentee trillions of dollars of mortgages in the credit derivatives market. A prime broker, like a Bear Stearns, lends money to the hedge funds, and yet these prime brokers or investment banks are themselves leveraged fifteen to twenty to one, again ignoring the trillions of dollars of exposure they have in the derivatives marketplace. The commercial banks that lend money to these investment banks are themselves leveraged from twelve to eighteen times, excluding not only their derivatives exposure, but ignoring all of their off-balance sheet highly leveraged activity.

In this example, there is only one relevant question. Who is watching the store? Who has invested real equity monies, and really cares if that mortgage is repaid on time? It appears in this example the answer is no one. The homeowner just walks away; the employees of the highly leveraged hedge fund get on the elevator that night, and just never return to work, and the investment and commercial banks get bailed out by the government. Such dramatic leverage in a financial system, by definition, has to cause enormous volatility throughout the world's economies, and generate frequent booms and busts. Everybody is betting big on the upside, with little to no concern about the downside.

Obama could return some sanity to this marketplace by insisting that participants have skin in the game, that is, have made substantial equity investments along with their debt investors. This would require great changes from the status quo, changes that would require difficult-to-pass, new legislation. It would be a much more stable world if the government prohibited all types of exotic mortgage products, including ARMS, option pay, negative amortization, and fifty-year repayment mortgages. If we insisted that all homebuyers put down a minimum 20 percent down payment in purchasing a home and sign a fixed-rate thirty year mortgage, for which they had the demonstrable income to qualify, we would eliminate much of the risk in the mortgage banking industry. We can argue whether hedge funds should be allowed to operate under no regulation and no reporting requirements, but for these purposes, it seems reasonable to require hedge funds to limit the use of leverage to a reasonable level and prevent small, poorly capitalized hedge funds from writing large insurance policies, or making substantial guarantees in the credit derivatives market that they could never honor in an economic downturn. Finally, commercial banks worldwide should be limited in the amount of leverage they can apply in purchasing assets, and the limitations should not be voluntary, but required by law through global negotiation. It makes absolutely no sense for our commercial banks to be conducting any business off-balance sheet, a lesson that was supposedly learned by our Enron experiences.

Lastly, and most seriously, the housing collapse and mortgage crisis uncovered the next time bomb that is ticking within our financial system. It is the global derivatives market. Currently, derivatives worldwide account for $400 trillion in counterparty contracts.[22] This book is not long enough to explain how derivatives work, but suffice it to say that they go almost completely unregulated and to a great degree unreported. They make fundamental financial analysis of a company's balance sheet and income statements meaningless.

The real damage done to the financial system by the derivatives market is not just that they have the potential to increase speculation, leverage and risk-taking, it is that they make the entire process of risk management and financial analysis meaningless. A single investor cannot determine the riskiness of a particular company or bank investment without understanding the company's derivatives exposure, and the government cannot allow any major commercial or investment bank to fail, given their importance as counterparties, in holding the whole derivative house of cards together. Banking reform is a huge undertaking, but one which, if Obama chooses to ignore it, will come back to haunt us in the very near future.

Chapter Four

THE BIGGEST PROBLEM: CORPORATE LOBBYING

I am in this race to tell the corporate lobbyists that their days of setting the agenda in Washington are over. I have done more than any other candidate in this race to take on lobbyists—and won. They have not funded my campaign, they will not run my White House, and they will not drown out the voices of the American people when I am president.[1]

The preceding quote from Barack Obama is fairly self-explanatory. But how big a deal is the power of special interests in Washington? As the title of this chapter hints, it is the key to all the reform his administration hopes to accomplish.

What do the current financial crisis, globalization, and global warming have in common? What do all three issues have to do with our inadequate healthcare system, the welfare of our working poor, or the financial security of our elderly? These rather disparate problems all have a direct impact on the health of the American economy. But what do they have in common?

Perhaps the table on the following page will make the answer more obvious.[2]

Yes, government policy on all the major issues we face is guided by powerful lobbyists who give money to your elected representatives,

MAJOR PROBLEM	CURRENT LOBBYING EFFORT
FINANCIAL MARKET CRISIS	Real Estate Lobby (e.g., National Association of Realtors), Mortgage Banking Lobby (e.g., Fannie Mae, Freddie Mac), Commercial Banking Lobby (e.g., J.P. Morgan, Bank of America), Investment Banking Lobby (e.g., Goldman Sachs, Morgan Stanley), Hedge Fund Lobbyists (e.g., Carlyle, Blackstone, KKR)
GLOBALIZATION	Business Lobby, including US Chamber of Commerce; Business Roudtable
GLOBAL WARMING	Oil and Gas Lobby (e.g., Exxon/Mobil), Automakers Lobby (General Motors, Ford Motor) Utility Lobby (e.g., Edison Electric Institute, Southern Company), Coal Lobby
HEALTHCARE	American Medical Association, American Hospital Association, Pharmaceutical Research & Manufacturers of America, HMO Lobby, Hospital Lobby, Blue Cross/Blue Shield
WORKING POOR AND MINIMUM WAGE	US Chamber of Commerce, Business Roundtable
SOCIAL SECURITY AND MEDICARE	AARP Lobby
WAR AND PEACE	Defense Lobby (e.g., Northrup Grumman, Boeing, Lockheed Martin)

who set the agenda for discussion, and who have been known to go so far as to write the final language in the bills Congress passes. In each case, the lobbyists are either causing the problem to go on unresolved, or, through their interference, are preventing the democratic system from reaching a resolution acceptable to all. If corporations' and the citizenry's objectives were perfectly aligned, there would be no need for corporate lobbyists. The fact that corporate lobbying exists means that its specific purpose is to pervert and corrupt the democratic process. It is for this reason that they have to go.

Almost every single major problem in America can be traced back to action by a local or federal government representative who is being unduly influenced and biased by lobbyists. Cigarette smoking in America: the tobacco lobby; inappropriate violence and sex in film and on television: the Hollywood lobby; corporate ownership of our news media: the media lobby; high drug prices: the pharmaceutical lobby; gambling: the casino lobby; housing prices collapsing: the real estate and mortgage lobby; financial institutions being bailed out: the Wall Street lobby.

Barack Obama recognizes this. He has refused to take money from lobbyists and from special interests during his campaign for the presidency. He has expressed his great disdain for lobbyists throughout the campaign, and has made lobbying his signature issue to address once in office.

Barack has a strong record of achievement in improving ethics in government. Below is a summary from his campaign's position paper, entitled "Plan to Change Washington," of the actions Obama has taken already to try to make government more transparent, less corrupt, less beholden to special interests, and more responsive to citizens:

FEDERAL ETHICS REFORM: Obama and Senator Feingold (D-WI) took on both parties and proposed ethics legislation that was described as the "gold standard" for reform. It was because of their leadership that ending subsidized corporate jet travel, mandating disclosure of lobbyists' bundling of contributions, and enacting strong new restrictions of lobbyist-sponsored trips became part of the final ethics bill that was signed into law. The *Washington Post* wrote in an editorial, "The final package is the strongest ethics legislation to emerge from Congress yet."

GOOGLE FOR GOVERNMENT: Americans have the right to know how their tax dollars are spent, but that information has been hidden from public view for too long. That's why Barack Obama and Senator Tom Coburn (R-OK) passed a law to create a Google-like search engine to allow regular people to approximately track federal grants, contracts, earmarks, and loans online. The *Chicago Sun-Times* wrote, "It would enable the public to see where federal money goes and how it is spent. It's a brilliant idea."

ILLINOIS REFORM: In 1998, Obama joined forces with former US Sen. Paul Simon (D-IL) to pass the toughest campaign finance law in Illinois history. The legislation banned the personal use of campaign money by Illinois legislators and banned most gifts from lobbyists. Before the law was passed, one organization ranked Illinois worst among fifty states for its campaign finance regulations.[3]

The sheer magnitude of the lobbying effort in Washington is almost beyond comprehension. Tens of thousands of people make their living in the profession. What was once a small national capital of a couple hundred thousand people is now a megalopolis of several million spread over thousands of square miles. There is no real industry in Washington, DC besides lobbying, and yet the pace of the city is frenetic with rush-hour traffic lasting from 5:00 a.m. to well past 11:00 p.m. You have to give it them—if nothing else, lobbyists are hardworking. Unfortunately, it is the work of undoing democracy in favor of corporate elitism.

Below is a table that demonstrates the magnitude and explosive growth over the last decade of the lobbying effort in the US. This does not include campaign contributions, just lobbying expense by special interests in Washington.[4]

1998	<>	$1.45 billion
1999	<>	$1.45 billion
2000	<>	$1.54 billion
2001	<>	$1.63 billion
2002	<>	$1.81 billion
2003	<>	$2.04 billion
2004	<>	$2.17 billion
2005	<>	$2.41 billion
2006	<>	$2.60 billion
2007	<>	$2.80 billion

The ten industries that spent the most on lobbying in 2007 are listed below.[5] To give you an idea of how pervasive lobbying is, over 630 corporations and organizations lobbied in 2007 in pharmaceutical and healthcare products alone.[6]

Industry	Number of Organizations	Total Lobbying (in millions)	Issues
PHARMACEUTICALS/ HEALTH PRODUCTS	630	$227.7	High Drug Prices; Health Care Costs
INSURANCE	240	$138.1	Healthcare Insurance Problems
ELECTRIC UTILITIES	320	$112.7	Global Warming
COMPUTERS/INTERNET	560	$110.4	2001 Internet Bubble
HOSPITALS/ NURSING HOMES	740	$91.1	Healthcare Problems
EDUCATION	1,190	$88.5	Education Problems
BUSINESS ASSOCIATIONS	210	$87.1	Wage Rates, Unions and Globalization
SECURITIES & INVESTMENT	290	$86.7	Financial Crisis
OIL & GAS	260	$82.6	Global Warming and Energy Costs
REAL ESTATE	420	$78.4	Housing and Mortgage Crash

It is not a coincidence that the computer/Internet industry was the prime beneficiary of the Internet and communications stock boom of the 1990s that led to the 2001 Internet bust, and that the real estate industry was behind the housing run-up of the last decade that led to the housing crash beginning in 2006. The securities and investments industry is behind the deregulation of the financial services industry that is the primary cause of the current financial crisis and credit crunch in America. The pharmaceutical, hospital, and insurance industries are the primary forces preventing any meaningful reform to our healthcare system. These industries are bribing our elected representatives to prevent them from enacting regulation and laws that would help protect the American public from the pain of boom and bust cycles. One can easily see a connection between the amount of money a particular industry gives Congress and the pain suffered by the American public.

Public Campaign published a list of forty of the biggest corporate campaign contributors and found that in aggregate they had contributed $150 million over a two-year election cycle. What was startling was that Public Campaign reported that this "investment" yielded tax breaks for these companies of over $55 billion.[7] These amounts of money sound so large and staggering that it is impossible to comprehend the success of these investments as a simple return on investment percentage (36,800 percent), but on average, a one dollar investment in an elected representative's campaign by a corporation yielded tax benefits to the company of $368.[8] While this ratio is staggeringly large, it does not begin to measure the total economic benefit these corporations garner through their campaign donations and lobbyists' efforts in addition to these tax subsidies.

In addition to corporate tax benefits such as direct tax credits, accelerated depreciation benefits, R&D tax credits, and other generous tax deductions, the enormous subsidies paid out to industry by Congress take on many forms, including price supports and subsidies, tariff protection, monopolistic profits, favorable patent protection, pension funding relief, anti-union legislation, and relief from onerous consumer, labor and environmental laws.

It is impossible to measure the magnitude of the harvest of big business's lobbying and campaign contribution efforts. But to demonstrate how the process works, let us examine each dollar of the wage savings that has resulted from big business's efforts at fighting wage increases in Washington. Let us assume that as a result of corporate efforts to break unions and encourage the immigration of inexpensive labor from abroad, the exporting of manufacturing jobs to developing countries, the outsourcing of jobs on the Internet, and the fight against raising the minimum wage, every employee in America is getting paid one dollar less per hour—a wealth transfer of $250 billion per year from the American worker directly to American business owners. A conservative estimate of the one dollar decline in wages, capitalized at twelve times earnings, shows that this would cause an approximate $3 trillion real increase in the market capitalizations of American business. It is not coincidental that the stock market has gone up some $3 trillion in real terms over the last seven years. Rather than congratulating business on the great job they have done opening new markets and developing new products, it appears that much of their success has come from lobbying their government to keep the cost of labor down, and in effect, transfer $3 trillion of wages from their workers to their shareholders. Of course, the actual impact may be much more than $1.00 per hour and may explain the entire aggregate increase in the stock market's value over the last forty years, a period of tough times for the American workers and unions.

This is just the impact for one dollar per hour in labor savings. When you include the savings that Corporate America has achieved through lobbying and campaign contributions for other activities, the numbers become truly startling. Hundreds of billions of dollars of corporate savings are achieved each year by preventing

Congress from enacting needed environmental legislation and by allowing companies to raid worker pensions and avoid worker health care liability. Corporations avoid hundreds of billions of dollars of potential product liability losses through Congress's appointment of pro-business judges to the courts. And corporations reap hundreds of billions of dollars of savings because Congress has loosened the clout of regulatory bodies such as OSHA, the FDA, the SEC and others.

Obama made exactly these points in a speech in Harrisburg during the Pennsylvania primary.[9] He cited that over $1 billion had been spent by pharmaceutical companies and healthcare companies over the last ten years to pressure Congress to keep their profit margins high, while Americans suffered with inadequate medical care. $400 million was spent by Wall Street and financial service industry commercial bank lobbyists to have Glass-Steagle overturned. This was a seventy-year-old law that had kept the activities of commercial banks separate from investment banks in order to protect depositors. The elimination of Glass-Steagle was one of the major reasons why the financial markets collapsed in 2007 and 2008, as there was no regulation to control risk and leverage in the financial sector.[10]

It is amazing that Americans do not rise up in revolt against such greed and injustice perpetrated by our government on behalf of our biggest corporations. That the average American has to work so hard to bring home so little to his family, and watch as our biggest corporations steal food from his family's mouths through their lobbying efforts, is unbelievable. Then there are the young Americans who fight in America's wars to protect a government that is so tragically corrupted by bribe-taking officials that it seems dedicated to protecting corporate greed above all else. One wonders, has the average American failed to understand the true damage that lobbyists are doing to our country, or has he realized the magnitude of the problem, but concluded there is nothing that can be done? Our major television networks, cable channels, and television news sources are now exclusively owned and run by big corporations. When was the last time you saw a news report on television critical of General Electric, Disney, or Time Warner, the major owners of our television news programs, or an investigative news program on the evils of corporate lobbying?

Just look at the farm lobby. Americans are under the misimpression that when we subsidize farmers and farm products, the money is going to small American farmers and their families. This isn't so. We give the milk lobby hundreds of millions per year. Ninety-five percent of it goes to very large corporate dairy producers. We give the sugar lobby billions of dollars per year, and almost all of it goes to the very large owners of corporate sugar plantations. And higher domestic prices due to price supports and tariff protection mean American consumers pay $15 billion more each year for farm produce than they should.[11] Environmentalists fought for ethanol subsidies to discourage global warming, and we end up with subsidies and price supports that have caused both corn prices and Archer Daniels Midland's stock price to double.

The Bush administration, prodded by the pharmaceutical lobby, touted its pharmaceutical benefit for the elderly as an act of compassion for all the citizens who are having trouble paying for their required drugs. In fact, all it did was transfer the exorbitant cost of buying these drugs from the elderly to a younger generation of Americans through increased taxes and increased government debt. The exorbitant prices charged by the pharmaceutical companies did not decline. In fact, they went up. The pharmaceutical companies were able to find a new deep pocket to pay ever-escalating prices of drugs—prices vastly higher than the cost of the same drugs in Canada and elsewhere.

There is a fundamental difference between a corporate special interest, which represents a single company or industry, and a group of citizens who organize themselves and wish to have a political influence in Washington. Unlike corporate lobbyists, there are millions of real people behind the AARP lobbying effort. This makes their lobbying more legitimate than corporate lobbyists, who are representing, not people, but legally created paper entities called corporations. But even well-meaning, people-backed organizations like the AARP can damage the public good with their lobbying efforts. The reason is simple. On a piece of legislation that directly affects the elderly, the AARP will turn out its members and its muscle and its money, while the average American, who may be negatively impacted by the proposed legislation is not represented in Washington. This is the problem with special interests. The special interest that has the most to gain is well represented in Washington, while the general interest of the people is not.

Obama was careful in his presidential campaign not to take any monies from lobbyists, PACS, or special interest groups. Of course, nothing prevented individual employees of large corporations or industries from donating to his campaign. And yet the majority of contributions from the industries went to his opponents. Here is where these individuals gave their money when aggregated by industry.[12]

HILLARY CLINTON WAS THE #1 DEMOCRATIC FUNDRAISER FROM THESE GROUPS:

Real Estate Industry
Banks/Wall Street
Healthcare/Pharmaceuticals Industry
Lobbyists
Lawyers
Casinos/Gambling Industry
Insurance Industry
Oil and Gas Industry
Tobacco
Large Contributors over $1,000

BARACK OBAMA WAS THE #1 DEMOCRATIC
FUNDRAISER FROM THESE GROUPS

Universities/Education
Retired Persons
Computer/Internet Businesses
Movie Industry
Music Business

While the table does not free Obama completely from charges that he may favor certain groups due to their generous giving, the disparity in the nature of the two campaigns' financial supporters reads like the funding of the never-ending battle of good versus evil. Hillary gets tobacco companies, the wealthy, drug companies, lawyers, lobbyists, and gamblers, and Barack gets artists, professors, and the elderly.

In his report on lobbying and the damage it can do to our country, Obama states that secrecy dominates government actions in Washington. The Bush administration has ignored public disclosure rules in the determination of many of our national policies such as Cheney's energy task force, comprised of oil and gas lobbyists who met secretly to develop our nation's energy policy.

The Bush administration has taken to an unprecedented extreme the practice of awarding government work without a competitive bid process. Halliburton, the company that Cheney headed before becoming vice president, has been the biggest beneficiary. Halliburton stock price appreciated eight fold from $6.00 per share to $48.00 per share during Cheney's time in the Bush administration. Halliburton was granted a no-bid contract to act as the prime contractor for all reconstruction work done in Iraq, and was offered a similar major no-bid contract to help rebuild New Orleans after hurricane Katrina. This is contrary to all stated government policy, and is probably illegal. How Congress and the American people allow this to occur is beyond common sense. It is difficult enough to keep government operations efficient given that there is no profit objective in the public sector. The first and only rule of awarding government contracts is that they must be competitive.

The gall of awarding noncompetitive contracts was exceeded only by the fact that Halliburton was the prime beneficiary. Everyone knew that Halliburton was Cheney's company. Of course, when he arrived in Washington and took the oath to become our vice president, he swore he had resigned from Halliburton, put all of his investment assets in a blind trust, and had broken ties with the company. The real truth probably never would have been uncovered, except for Cheney's bad luck and poor aim. As I'm sure you remember, Dick Cheney had an unfortunate weekend hunting trip where he ended up shooting a lawyer in the face with buckshot. The story was picked up on all of the major news networks, mostly for its entertainment value. Little was made of the fact that Cheney did not report the incident for some twenty-four hours. And nothing was made of the real news uncovered: the people Cheney was hunting with were the owners and the founders of Halliburton. He had not broken any ties, he was not acting blindly, he just had the unfortunate luck to errantly shoot a Halliburton lawyer in the face. Americans who understood felt as if they had been shot in the face, too.

When an activity becomes as unjust and corrupt as corporate lobbying and the vast corporate bribes being given to our elected officials, sometimes nothing more is needed to correct it than shining a bright light on the activity. Obama is very specific about what he intends to do.[13] He will create a centralized Internet database that is accessible to everyone and that presents campaign finance information and lobbying reports in a searchable, sortable, and downloadable format. He will require independent monitoring of ethics rules in Congress, and will fight for an independent watchdog agency to oversee the investigation of congressional ethics violations. Obama supports the public financing of electoral campaigns, in combination with the use of free television and radio time as a way to reduce the influence of moneyed special interests and elections.

Further increasing transparency, Obama will create a public contracts and influence database that will disclose how much federal contractors spend on lobbying, what contracts they get, and how well they complete them. He will see that any tax breaks or earmarks for corporate recipients are also publicly available on the Internet in an easily searchable format. Obama will end the practice of the government's no-bid contracts by requiring that nearly all contract orders over $25,000 be competitively bid and awarded.[14]

In Congress, bills to satisfy lobbyists that are harmful to the public are often rushed through in the dead of night. As president, Obama will not sign any non-emergency bill without giving the American public at least five days to review the bill and comment. Any earmark for pork barrel spending attached to a bill will have to be accompanied by the name of the legislator who asked for the earmark, along with a written justification.[15]

It is Obama's hope that as he cleans up the federal government and makes it more transparent and honest, he will encourage more Americans to reclaim their right as citizens in a participatory democracy. He will insist that his cabinet officials hold periodic national town hall meetings. All White House communications about regulatory policymaking between persons outside government and White House staff shall be a matter of public record. All executive branch departments and rule-making agencies shall conduct their business in public.[16]

Obama intends to close the revolving door that allows former government employees to work as lobbyists, then rotate back into government. In an Obama administration, political appointees in the government will not be allowed to work on any regulation or contract related to their prior employer for two years. And no political appointee will be able to leave government service and lobby the government for the remainder of the administration.[17]

Americans have known for some time that big corporations

were getting special deals by bribing our elected representatives, but so far have chosen to ignore it. Given the recent housing crash and the current financial crisis in our nation, more Americans will come to understand that this complete failure of our market-based economy and the most sophisticated financial marketplace in the world could not have occurred without manipulation of our Congress and President by corporate and banking lobbyists. Congressmen and presidents were, in effect, paid to look the other way, to minimize or repeal regulation that had previously protected the homeowners of America and the health of our economy through the proper functioning of our markets. When this story is understood fully, the American people will hopefully be motivated to take whatever actions are necessary to clean up Washington and reclaim their government.

Perhaps the clearest vision Obama has given us during the campaign of how strongly he feels about the damage that lobbyists are doing to this nation, and some of the steps he plans to take to correct it, can be found in his Cooper Union speech from March 27, 2008.[18]

In the speech, Obama squarely lays the blame for the housing and financial crisis enveloping the country at the feet of Washington lobbyists and the elected representatives who corrupted the system by refusing to pass necessary regulation in exchange for bribes. Over the last twenty years, Obama said, our economy has undergone a fundamental shift due to the rapid pace of technological change and globalization. For the sake of the common good, the country needed to adapt new regulations to keep markets competitive and fair. Instead, aided by a legal, but corrupt, bargain in which campaign money all too often shaped policy and watered down oversight, Washington dismantled the old regulatory framework and put nothing in its place. Obama cites deregulation of the telecommunications industry as leading to massive overinvestment and subsequent layoffs and bankruptcies. He believes companies like Enron took advantage of partial deregulation of the electricity industry and engaged in accounting fraud to improve their profits and gouge their customers by manipulating the retail price of electricity. This didn't happen by accident, and it did not happen, according to Obama, by the invisible hand of the free markets. Rather, it was the hand of industry lobbyists tilting the playing field in Washington. Obama went on to say that the current financial crisis is a result of deregulation of the financial sector, led by a lobbying effort more interested in facilitating mergers than creating an efficient regulatory framework.

Obama's basic point in his speech was that we are all in this together. A Wall Street firm can improve its profits in the short run by hiring lobbyists to convince Congress to lower its effective tax rate. But if the lobbyists' actions, encouraged by and paid for by big corporations, big banks, and Wall Street are not in America's interests and do not improve Americans.welfare, then in the end even Wall Street will suffer.

Obama has spoken often of his desire to re-engage the American people in democracy. He has suggested town hall meetings with his cabinet members and broadcasts of important administration conferences over the Internet or on C-SPAN to ensure openness and transparency. He understands that the way to battle corruption, both by corporate special interests and your elected representatives, is to open the process of governing to the people. It is the people who should be deciding issues important to them, not some government bureaucrat, and certainly not some lobbyist.

What better way to involve all of our citizens than to ask them to vote once a month using their cell phones or the Internet on important issues? This form of direct democracy would not even have to be binding. But it would mean that the government could ask Americans their positions on the war, the deficit, healthcare alternatives, trade policies, the minimum wage, and so on, and the results would inform the decisions of our representatives in Congress and in the White House. The results would be available instantaneously, and could be analyzed according to the state, city, congressional district or whatever level of detail is required.

There would be two immediate benefits. First, elected representatives would know immediately what the nation on the whole, and their own constituents in particular, think about an issue. This would make the will of the people awfully difficult to ignore, especially in an election year. Second, such a system would lessen the power of our elected representatives and the Washington lobbyists intent on delivering special favors to their clients. As more power is given directly to the people of this country, corrupt lobbying will become increasingly difficult to pull off. The more decision-makers there are, the harder it is to bribe all of them. While Obama has not suggested such a nationwide poll, he would be well advised to consider it.

The old argument for allowing corporate lobbying to influence our government can be summarized by the expression, "what's good for GM is good for America." If this were ever true, it no longer is today. Globalization has made GM a world power. They may be headquartered in Detroit, but their manufacturing facilities, their employees, many of their executives, their revenues, and their profits are spread throughout the globe. GM, like every American chartered corporation, has only one objective: to maximize profits. For GM, this obviously means global profits. The courts in the United States have made it clear that corporations' managements and boards of directors' sole responsibility is to maximize returns for their shareholders. There is no room for community, environmental, charitable, employee, neighborhood, or patriotic concerns. Profit maximization is it.

So when GM thinks about how to best maximize its profits, it cannot be thinking about what is best for America, American workers, or the American consumer. It has become detached from America. If firing an American worker and hiring a worker in China increases its profits, it must do it. If relocating an assembly line from Detroit to Shanghai increases profits, it must do it. If closing all the car plants in Flint, leaving the city open to crime and decay, improves corporate profitability, it must do it. If GM can find a legal way to increase production at a lower cost, even if it means increased pollution, it must do it. And if it can sell an inferior product with no risk to GM's reputation, it must do it.

It is fascinating to think that most of our problems today are caused by legal entities we created that are nothing more than fabrications of our minds. I am speaking of corporations and governments. Both have demonstrated the enormous potential to do good for their creators, humans on this planet, but both have also grown in power and stature, to the point that they cause harm to the very people who created them. In aggregate, these legal entities, corporations and governments, certainly do more good than bad. The challenge for the next generation will be to rein in these powerful inventions of mankind to assure that they are doing our good work here on earth. Both the government and corporations ultimately have to be responsible to the people who created them, and humans have to quit acting like slaves to them.

Throughout Obama's books and speeches, he argues determinedly that the root cause of our problems is the undue influence on our government of special interests, primarily corporate special interests. Early in his campaign, he was slow to hammer this point home publicly, but as he entered the general election he made it the core of many of his campaign presentations. He began to name names, citing the HMO lobby for slowing healthcare reform and expressing concern over Exxon/Mobil's $40 billion of annual profits as gas prices rose. Of all the problems Obama will inherit on day one of his presidency, stopping the special interests will have to be his first priority.

Chapter Five

GLOBALIZATION AND JOBS

In the end, I believe that expanding trade and breaking down barriers between countries is good for our economy and for our security, for American consumers and American workers. . . . [Globalization] is a technological revolution that is fundamentally changing the world's economy, producing winners and losers along the way. The question is not whether we can stop it, but how we respond to it. It's not whether we should protect our workers from competition, but what we can do to fully enable them to compete against workers all over the world.

These strong words in support of international trade and globalization are from an OpEd Obama published in the *Chicago Tribune* on June 30, 2005, entitled "Why I Oppose CAFTA." They come from a man, well-traveled, who has witnessed how closed countries and economies around the world can stagnate without the new technologies and fresh ideas that international trade presents. International trade brings openness, and with it a demand for transparency and good government. Businessmen cannot trade effectively with dictatorial governments who can change laws on a whim and nationalize industries overnight. And yet, as the title of the article indicates, Obama was raising his voice here in *opposition* to a free-trade agreement. Obama believes that trade agreements must address not only the corporate bottom line, but also critical issues of fairness, such as labor, environmental, and consumer safety.

The basic theory behind international trade is that it must benefit both countries or else they wouldn't participate. This is reinforced by David Ricardo's work in the eighteenth century on the comparative advantage of trade, which says that trade should benefit both parties because fewer man-hours and resources are expended to create greater amounts of goods and services.[1] But nowhere in Ricardo's work does it say that all parties within a country must benefit from trade equally, or even that all must benefit. Within each country that trades, there can be winners and losers.

While most economists today swear by Ricardo's work, many of its statements about the benefits of comparative advantage have been made obsolete by the modern world we live in. The free flow of capital, ideas, and labor skills across countries makes it much less likely that international trade would be necessary, or would bring much benefit to the parties involved. In Ricardo's time, Italians might make a better shoe and thus export it to the world, but today, Chinese do not have to import Italian shoes; they can learn shoemaking skills themselves and produce them domestically with little trade from Italy.

Most economists would swear that international trade benefits a country. But empirically, this has never been proven. A recent research study conducted by this author concluded that international trade was relatively unimportant in predicting the wealth of nations once more important variables such as property rights, democratic institutions, and the rule of law were included in the analysis.

The trade Obama is most concerned with is that which costs jobs in America and depresses wages here. Primarily, this is trade with developing countries who have a much lower wage structure due to their much lower cost of living. This includes trade with China, India, Brazil, Mexico, the rest of Latin America, Eastern Europe, and Southeast Asia and Oceania. Please recognize, this trade is not growing rapidly because of some grand Ricardian scheme in which they make better shoes and we make better computer chips. No, it is occurring because the countries are so poor, and their cost of living so low, that they have a much lower wage structure than America. It is not a comparative advantage, it is a direct advantage—lower wages. Because of these lower wages, these developing countries can produce shoes, apparel, and even electronic chips cheaper than us. If there is any comparative advantage to the ensuing trade, it is that more labor-intensive industries will likely shift overseas sooner than less labor-intensive industries. But as long as their wages are lower than ours, there is nothing to prevent all American industry from eventually moving abroad. In fact, that is what I predict would happen until the cost of living and wages rise in the developing country.

And it is not going to stop anytime soon. The jobs moving abroad are not limited to low-skilled manufacturing jobs; the Internet allows highly skilled engineers, accountants, medical technicians, and computer programmers in developing countries to compete directly for work globally. If you are a computer programmer in the United States and earning $120,000 a year, you have probably noticed that a great deal of work is being outsourced to India, where a comparable programmer earns $30,000 a year. You may be hopeful that the increase in programming assignments to India will eventually drive wages up and protect your salary, but don't be. No matter how much programming work gets shipped off to India, the programmer there will always earn approximately one quarter of what programmers in the United States earn.

This is not because they are less productive than their American counterparts. It is simply because it costs less to live in India than in the United States. As a matter of fact, it costs approximately 75 percent less to live a comparable life in India.[2] So from a cost-of-living and quality of life perspective, the $30,000 Indian salary is exactly equivalent to the $120,000 American's salary. This cost-of-living advantage, which is reflected in the lower wages in India, is not going to go away anytime soon.

You see, Indian programmers can work as hard as they want and be as productive as they want, but until the entire Indian population pulls themselves out of poverty and attains a better standard of living and higher wage structure, the cost of living in India will not increase. The cost of living for the programmer in India is not determined by him, but by what he has to pay others there to work for him and provide him food, clothing and shelter. The bottom line is that the wage advantage that the developing world has over the United States will continue for quite some time.

Obama understands this. He knows that globalization and international trade are here to stay. But he also understands that international trade is not benefiting all parties, nor is it necessarily fair to all parties. America is a country of laws and principles and borders. Nothing says that we have to trade with other countries of the world. Just because it benefits those other countries does not mean that America has to enter into trade agreements. Similarly, America does not have to send troops to every country of the world that is fighting for its independence from tyranny and for democratic freedom. There is not some natural law or economic theory that forces us to trade around the world. If we find that a majority of our people are not benefiting from such trade, it can and should be stopped.

For example, it's fairly obvious to all that the real losers in American world trade are our blue-collar manufacturing workers. With greater technology and mechanization, their relatively low-skilled jobs can easily be transferred to lower wage countries. But that doesn't mean that we have to do so. Before we jump at trading with low-wage, sometimes dictatorial or tyrannical third world countries, we have to ask ourselves whether the access to cheaper T-shirts and shoes is worth destroying the fabric of American society, namely our egalitarian middle class.

Think of it this way. What if, rather than "discovering" developing countries like China, India, and Vietnam with large numbers of underutilized and poorly paid manual workers, we discovered a new planet in the solar system that was populated solely by unemployed doctors? Millions of them. Is there some grand economic theory that says we would have to trade with such a planet? Surely our country would benefit in aggregate; the cost of medical care would drop precipitously, along with salaries of doctors living here. I can assure you, the AMA would be against such trade. We as a society would have to make a decision as to how badly we would like to punish our doctors and force them to compete with this new, never ending supply of medical practitioners and weigh it against the benefits of lower medical costs. I hope our society would attempt to find a solution that provided work for the starving alien doctors on the other planet, improved our welfare by lowering medical costs, and, most importantly, provided some method of easing the pain of Earth's doctors as they faced unemployment, job dislocations, and higher retraining and relocation costs.

Obama comments on this, saying, "But the larger problem is what's missing from our prevailing policy on trade and globalization—namely, meaningful assistance for those who are not reaping its benefits and a plan to equip American workers with the skills and support they need to succeed in a twenty-first century economy. . . . So far, almost all of our energy and almost all of these trade agreements are about making life easier for the winners of globalization, while we do nothing as life gets harder for American workers."[3]

Some think it is unnatural, unnecessary, or even un-American to hold out a helping hand to workers that have been displaced by globalization like Obama is recommending. Nothing could be further from the truth. Literally trillions of dollars of value and benefit accrue to American consumers and businesses as a result of these international trade agreements. We buy beautiful garments for one tenth of what they used to cost, receive valuable business services at an 80 percent discount off what Americans would charge, and are rapidly approaching being able to pay $100 for a laptop computer. Certainly, as a society, we can give some of this gain back to those whose lives have been torn asunder by global-ized trade.

Obama adds, "But this is about more than displaced workers. Our failure to respond to globalization is causing a race to the bottom that means lower wages and stingier health and retiree benefits for all Americans. It's causing a squeeze on middle-class families who are working harder but making even less and struggling to stay afloat in this new economy. As one downstate (Illinois) worker told me during a recent visit, 'It doesn't do me much good if I'm saving a dollar on a T-shirt at Wal-Mart, but don't have a job.'"[4]

Globalization has been a direct attack, not only on the middle class in America and its manufacturing workers, but also on unions. When we force our workers to compete with a billion underemployed workers around the world, such a gross surplus of labor cannot be handled by any free market system on its own.

Obama has real plans to strengthen Americans' ability to organize into unions. From his campaign policy statement, I quote:

ENSURE FREEDOM TO UNIONIZE: Obama believes that workers should have the freedom to choose whether to join a union without harassment or intimidation from their employers. Obama cosponsored and is a strong advocate for the Employee Free Choice Act (EFCA), a bipartisan effort to assure that workers can exercise their right to organize. He will continue to fight for EFCA's passage and sign it into law.

FIGHT ATTACKS ON WORKERS' RIGHT TO ORGANIZE: Obama has fought the Bush National Labor Relations Board (NLRB) efforts to strip workers of their right to organize. He is a cosponsor of legislation to overturn the NLRB's "Kentucky River" decisions classifying hundreds of thousands of nurses, construction, and professional workers as "supervisors" who are not protected by federal labor laws.

PROTECT STRIKING WORKERS: Obama supports the right of workers to bargain collectively and strike if necessary. He will work to ban the permanent replacement of striking workers, so workers can stand up for themselves without worrying about losing their livelihoods.[5]

There are Americans who see unionization as bad. If it is bad, it is a necessary evil. One only need look back at the hardships workers faced before unions to understand their importance. Some workers today choose not to join unions, but they must realize that the wage levels they are paid, the work environment and hours they enjoy, the mandatory overtime payments and vacations, and the protection against workplace injuries all result from hard-fought battles by unions.

Just like international trade, if Mexicans are willing to work here in the United States for $8.00 an hour and do the work that an American was being paid $14.00 an hour to do, the country, in aggregate, should be better off. But such a system of imported labor is truly unfair to the American worker. The Mexican bids for work and then sends a large percentage of his wages home to his family in Mexico, which has a dramatically lower cost of living. The American worker doesn't have a chance. They cannot accept, nor should they, the same low wages a Mexican might, because they have to raise their family in a much higher cost of living environment here in America.

There has been much discussion as to how to end this illegal immigration wave into America. To date, very little has been done. Billions of dollars are planned to be spent on building a fence with Mexico. There need be no such fence. There need be no mass deportation. One simple act can solve the entire problem. The Social Security administration says that approximately 4 percent of the 430 million Social Security numbers that employers report to them do not match any valid numbers they have ever issued. This represents the approximately 16 million people who are working and making Social Security payments to accounts that don't exist, and thus will never see these benefits accrue to anyone. Is it a coincidence that this is almost exactly equal to the estimated number of illegal aliens in our country?

The Bush administration, halfheartedly, under great pressure from Americans concerned about illegal immigration, announced that the Social Security Administration will send out letters to the 16 million mismatches, and if there are no responses within three months, will contact their employers. A circuit court initially ruled that this was unconstitutional, arguing that Social Security's own records were not accurate enough to prove that completely legal Americans wouldn't be threatened by the action. The Social Security Administration has responded to the court injunction by demonstrating that their records are accurate. They have argued that if they sent a letter by mistake to a legal worker, they would be doing him a great service by straightening out his Social Security account and assuring his payments were accruing properly toward his retirement account. Obama wants to remove incentives for illegals to enter the country by cracking down on employers who hire undocumented immigrants. Obama has championed a proposal to create a system so employers can verify that their employees are legally eligible to work in the US.[6]

With regard to immigration, Obama believes the time to fix our broken immigration system is now. He is in favor of stronger enforcement at the border and at the workplace. He has properly identified the magnitude of the problem, and said that the undocumented population is exploding. The number of undocumented immigrants in the country has increased more than 40 percent since 2000, and every year more than a half a million people illegally enter the country. Obama recognizes that immigration raids are ineffective, netting only 3,600 arrests in 2006.[7]

Obama's priority is to stop the current way of illegal immigration into the United States, and then deal compassionately and fairly with the illegal immigrants who are already living here. If the flood of new immigrants can be slowed considerably, Obama believes that those currently living here, over time, can be effectively absorbed into the population and the economy.

Obama recognizes the importance of education in easing the negative impacts of globalization on workers. "If we are to promote free and fair trade—and we should—then we must make a national commitment to prepare every child in America with the education they need to compete in the new economy; to provide retraining and wage insurance so even if you lose your job you can train for another; to make sure worker retraining helps people without getting them caught in bureaucracy; that it helps service workers as well as manufacturing workers and encourages people to re-enter the workforce as soon as possible."[8]

If developing countries with their low wages are going to do most of the unskilled work in the world, that obviously frees up many American laborers to do something else. The question of course, is what is that something else? Ideally, America, the more advanced country, would have a better educated and more skilled workforce than the developing countries, and would do jobs that required greater skill and education. But is probably not reasonable to think that, even with education and training opportunities, Americans will become highly skilled or educated. There will always be a significant number of Americans who remain relatively unskilled, because they are currently being left behind due to rapid changes brought about by globalization and the mechanization of a technologically advanced world. One can hope that their children will see the benefits of getting an education and apply themselves diligently to prepare for higher-skilled jobs. This is happening to a great degree. But its effect is not universal.

The story of America right now, and for some time to come, is one where children, especially in rural America, grow up to take one of two very different paths. Either they go off to college, take a high-paying job in the city, and never return home, or they take a low-paying job close to their parents in the town where they grew up. While both lifestyles have appeal, the rural American, the non-global American, will be put under greater and greater stress economically to provide for his family. Already, it is common in rural America for both the husband and wife to work full-time, and it is not uncommon for either one or both of them to hold two jobs. Both parents working sixty or more hours a week begs the obvious question, who is watching the children? These children, with so little parental supervision, have little chance of developing the necessary skills they will need to compete. Our policies may be making our people and our country poorer in the long run, not richer, and we compound the problem by neglecting the next generation.

One simple change could make all the difference to these families and to their children's outlook for success. Were we to raise the minimum wage in this country from $5.85 an hour to $10.00 an hour, the change in our society would be enormous. Right now, at minimum wage, a single mother can work two jobs, or both members of a young couple can work full-time, and the family can still be living in or near poverty. You cannot raise a family on $6.00 an hour. If we increase the minimum wage to $10.00 an hour, one parent could work sixty hours a week, earning $30,000 a year, and the couple could afford to spend much more time raising their children.

While he has not specified a suggested level for the new minimum, Obama has come out in favor of increasing the minimum wage above the $7.25 per hour it is due to increase to in 2009, and keeping it pegged to inflation, so workers do not lose purchasing power in the future. It is interesting to note that if the minimum wage in 1963 had just kept up with general CPI inflation, the minimum wage today would be close to $9.00 an hour. $10.00 an hour may seem high to some, but many local municipalities have negotiated exactly that level of wages for all contract work done with them. If Obama is successful in subsidizing healthcare for those on minimum wage, $10.00 an hour might be the difference between being able to provide for one's family or not.

Of course there are those who say that such a wage increase

would be devastating to the American economy. This just isn't true. Low-wage labor is not as important a key to success in most American industries as you might think. Law firms, doctors offices, computer companies, and car companies would go on, business as usual. Most jobs that are highly dependent on low wages have already been outsourced or moved overseas. For those industries in America that depend on low-wage labor, such as the fast food industry, the nursing home industry, home healthcare, and janitorial and cleaning services, the impact would be much less negative than many other factors. And remember that a better paid worker is a potential customer, so there is a positive impact as well.

For example, if McDonald's were forced to pay its workers a fully loaded $10.00 an hour instead of $6.00 an hour, something like 80 percent of their employees would see a dramatic increase in pay. But if all fast food companies were facing the same increase in labor costs, it would be logical to assume that they would all just pass that higher cost on to the consumer. There's no reason to believe that McDonald's profits would be harmed at all. The consumer would have to pay more for his hamburgers. But it may not be as bad as you think.

Only McDonald's has accurate figures on what percentage of a hamburger's cost is low price labor. But if you think of the cost of meat, the cost of growing the lettuce and tomatoes, the cost of shipping the raw ingredients, the cost of the building and the value of the real estate in the parking lot, it's hard to imagine that the sixty seconds of low-cost labor in each hamburger adds much to the cost of the hamburger you purchase. If sixty seconds is all it takes to assemble and sell a hamburger, and we double wages from $6.00 to $12.00, that means the minute of hard labor going into the hamburger costs us $0.10 more. If we assume there is additional low-wage labor further upstream in the meat processing, farming, or trucking effort, and all of this cost is passed on to the consumer, than the price of a hamburger might increase from $2.00 to $2.20.

This, certainly, is much less impact on hamburger pricing than most people would have expected. Most Americans would be glad to pay 10 percent more for their hamburgers, if it meant knowing that their fellow Americans could work their way out of poverty, feed their families, pay their rent, and have enough time left at the end of the day to show their children how much they truly loved them.

Not all of this increase in compensation has to come through higher minimum wages. The earned income tax credit, which Obama supports, has been very effective in raising the incomes of the poorest Americans without artificially distorting the wage structure in low-wage labor-intensive industries.

While Obama has been an advocate of free trade, he sees the need to make sure that it is fairly regulated. The original trade agreements written primarily by the law firms of big corporations were very careful to derive protections for international property, intellectual property rights, and the enforcement of contracts necessary to do business effectively. They were almost completely devoid of any regulation to protect the consumer, the environment, or the worker. Obama has supported trade agreements with countries like Peru that have been properly structured to include these provisions, but is insistent that trade agreements like NAFTA be renegotiated to include such provisions.

Obama understands that we cannot allow trade with countries like China if they are not going to respect the rights of workers and consumers. Recently we have seen the threat to our economy and to our people of allowing unsafe Chinese toys into America. Chinese pharmaceutical products are being produced that not only do not include the stated levels of required medications and ingredients, but are riddled and contaminated with poisonous products, often added intentionally to the production process because they have lower production costs. While we can crack down on the Chinese government and ask them to tighten their production standards, the Chinese may find it very difficult to do so given that they have given such a free rein to much of their industry in order for it to grow rapidly outside the control of any federal regulation.

Obama wants to include tough environmental protections in all future trade agreements. It doesn't make much sense in a world of global warming and other global environmental impacts to export highly polluting industries overseas and not expect ramifications to America. We can export energy intensive businesses and industries to China, but if they are utilizing coal as their basic energy source, the entire world suffers the consequences of higher concentrations of carbon dioxide and greater global warming. We send dirty chemical operations to border towns in Mexico, and then act surprised when their effluent runs downstream into the ocean and washes up on our beaches in San Diego. We would like to see Brazil and other tropical rain forest countries cease cutting trees in their forests, but what authority do we have to ask them to slow their development when America has cut down 95 percent of our forests for our own development?

Globalization is an enormously complex issue. Obama knows this, and he recognizes that in America, there are both winners and losers due to globalization. He believes in the decency of average Americans, and believes that if big business and big corporations were not unduly influencing our elected representatives in Washington, average Americans would want to share the benefits of international trade more equally with those who are harmed by it. Obama would like to see Americans support plans that allow for better training of unskilled workers in America and that open up more educational opportunities for their children, including college for those who cannot afford it, and he would like to see health benefits that are portable and can be carried with a person from job to job, thus making job loss and displacement easier on Americans. If explained properly, most Americans would be in favor of dramatically raising the minimum wage. It is good for America. It is good for our families. And given the unusual economic forces brought to bear on the American worker by globalization, it is the right thing to do.

Chapter Six

GLOBAL WARMING AND ENERGY POLICY

Just about every scientist outside the White House believes climate change is real, it's serious, and is accelerated by the continued release of carbon dioxide. If the prospect of melting ice caps, rising sea levels, changing weather patterns, more frequent hurricanes, more violent tornadoes, endless dust storms, decaying forests, dying coral reefs, and increases in respiratory illness and insect-borne diseases—if all that doesn't constitute a serious threat, I don't know what does.[1]

Possibly no other event will have greater impact on our long-term growth than global warming. If we ignore it, the dislocations to our weather patterns, droughts, food shortages, mass migrations, and possible armed conflicts could cost trillions of dollars. If we choose to address it, but are not careful, we could kill the golden goose of industrial development and cause the third world to languish in poverty for decades to come. The culprit of warming, carbon dioxide, is also one of the major byproducts of industrialization. The challenge is to find a new way of approaching the problem that does not cause a direct tradeoff—less warming for less development in the world.

Obama made it perfectly clear who was to blame for the fact that the United States had not developed a plan to deal with global warming and energy independence. In a speech he gave in October of 2007 in Portsmouth, New Hampshire, he blamed the Washington political climate, and the corporate special interests who control it, for what has happened to the planet:

> . . . it's also a failure of our politics that pre-dates the presidency of George W. Bush. We have heard promises about energy independence from every single US President since Richard Nixon—Republicans and Democrats. We've heard proposals to curb our use of fossil fuels in nearly every State of the Union address since the oil embargo of 1973. Back then we imported about a third of our oil. Now we import over half. Back then global warming was just the theory of a few scientists. Now it is a fact that threatens our very existence.
>
> The truth is, our energy problem has become an energy crisis because no matter how well-intentioned the promise—no matter how bold the proposal—they all fall victim to the same Washington politics that has only become more divided and dishonest; more timid and calculating; more beholden to the powerful interests that have the biggest stake in the status quo."[2]

Obama's plan has four parts, and his long-term goal is to reduce all carbon emissions by 80 percent by the year 2050.[3] Obama will 1) Introduce a market-based cap and trade system to limit carbon emissions; 2) Encourage renewable and alternative energy use; 3) Emphasize conservation and improve energy efficiency; and 4) Reestablish America as the global leader in global warming negotiations.[4] Let us look in more detail at Obama's proposals in each area.

1. INTRODUCE A MARKET-BASED CAP AND TRADE SYSTEM TO LIMIT CARBON EMISSIONS

Obama intends to introduce a cap and trade system similar to what is currently being utilized in Europe. In effect, companies bid for the right to pollute each ton of CO_2 emissions they create. This adds the true cost of production to CO_2 emitters, but rather than forcing them to stop, allows them to buy rights to pollute in the market, thus assuring that the least expensive path to CO_2 reduction is followed. From Obama's plan to reduce carbon emissions 80 percent by 2050. I quote:

CAP AND TRADE: Obama's cap and trade system will require all pollution credits to be auctioned. A 100 percent auction ensures that all polluters pay for every ton of emissions they release, rather than giving these emission rights away to coal and oil companies . . .

CONFRONT DEFORESTATION AND PROMOTE CARBON SEQUESTRATION: Obama will develop domestic incentives that reward forest owners, farmers, and ranchers when they plant trees, restore grasslands, or undertake farming practices that capture carbon dioxide from the atmosphere.[5]

Obama's cap and trade system is a market-based approach to the problem.[6] This should be good news. A cap and trade system utilizes market prices and market concepts such as supply and demand to achieve reductions in carbon dioxide emissions on the most cost-efficient basis possible. But make no mistake about it, by making producers pay to pollute under such a system, you have increased the recognized cost of production. An economist would say you have actually shifted the externality cost of higher global temperatures from the planet to the producer. This is good, as he can now try to control it. But a very real cash cost will accrue to the producers under such a cap and trade system, and it is only natural to assume that they will try to pass these increased costs on to consumers.

Many consider such an imposition on producers to be a new tax. Under the Obama plan, new government revenues from such a cap and trade system will partly go to encourage energy efficiency, and thus further reduce global warming, but the majority of the revenue increase will go to paying for Obama's healthcare plan.

There is an alternative. Obama could utilize a cap and trade system, but rather than taking the hundred billion dollars of proceeds as a tax to fund healthcare proposals, he could redistribute it right back to industry. The cap and trade system is supposed to stop global warming, not raise new tax revenues for other governmental policies. A simple equal distribution to all industry participants would have the effect of making carbon emission more costly to the individual polluter without adding to the cost basis of industry in general. A portion of the proceeds might also be used to give further incentives to industry to increase their energy, efficiency, and conservation, and thus more quickly reduce their carbon footprint. When the government collected hundreds of billions of dollars from the tobacco industry, the money ended up going to sidewalks and roads and to pay for higher government salaries, but little actually went to the planned anti-smoking campaigns activists envisioned.

Critics of the cap and trade method of reducing carbon emissions have claimed that such a system is nothing more than allowing polluters to pay for the right to pollute. At the micro level, at the individual firm level, this is correct. But in aggregate, across the entire society, the total amount of carbon dioxide emissions will decrease exactly in proportion to the amount of pollution rights that have been sold. If you want CO_2 emissions to decline by 10 percent in one year, you simply issue 10 percent fewer pollution rights. The true cost to industry will be determined once they bid for those rights in an auction. And, because the system is market-based, the reduction will be accomplished on the most cost efficient basis possible. In other words, you are telling industry the amount you want carbon emissions reduced for the year, and the cap and trade system is allowing industry to make the least expensive reductions first.

But the cap and trade system, like all market systems, has its shortfalls. Markets are not necessarily ethical. They are just efficient. Suppose under a global cap and trade system of carbon reduction, developing countries like Brazil are paid not to cut down their rain forests. We all know that trees ingest carbon dioxide and emit oxygen through photosynthesis. It may be more cost efficient, in an attempt to reduce global warming, to stop the cutting of global forests rather than restrict the burning of fossil fuels. From an economic perspective and a market perspective, this seems reasonable. The world's planned reduction in global carbon emissions is achieved at the least cost. But what does this mean? In effect, the rich countries of the world are paying the less developed countries of the world cash payments to encourage them not to develop, to remain small farm agrarian and forest dwellers. This doesn't seem right. And it is not right. Economists must realize that market solutions, while efficient, do not always lead to morally correct solutions. The developing world, must be given the opportunity to grow and advance, and the cost of containing global warming must be born by those who have caused it to date, the advanced countries of the world.

A major benefit of a cap and trade system for reducing carbon dioxide emissions is that it encourages technological innovation to solve the problem. Throughout his writings, Obama emphasizes technological innovation as the key to solving some of our most complex problems: "If we want an innovation economy . . . then we have to invest in our future innovators by doubling federal funding of basic research over the next five years, training 100,000 more engineers and scientists over the next four years, or providing research grants to the most outstanding early career researchers in the country."[7]

Cap and trade systems encourage technological innovation,

because they put a real cost on carbon dioxide emissions. An entrepreneur who can develop a technological method of eliminating carbon dioxide emissions will be greatly rewarded under such a cap and trade system. By properly identifying the cost, the cap and trade approach encourages smart entrepreneurs and scientists to eliminate the problem altogether, hopefully at little new cost. This is Obama's stated position.[8]

One negative aspect of a cap and trade system is that, to some, extent it hides the cost of cleaning up carbon dioxide emissions from the consumer. While the cost may indeed be passed through to the consumer in the form of higher prices, it will not be identified as such, and the consumer will not be able to judge how much he is paying for reducing the risk of global warming. To put this in perspective, imagine a more direct approach. Imagine if, rather than a cap and trade system, Obama was suggesting a $2.00 per gallon increase in the cost of gasoline in order to reduce global warming; or alternatively, imagine if he were recommending a 1 percent increase in the sales tax to clean up carbon dioxide emissions. There would obviously be much less enthusiasm for such plans. Americans may want their government to do something about global warming, but like most problems we face, it is not clear that they wish to experience any sacrifice in order to attain the goal of lower carbon emissions.

2. ENCOURAGE RENEWABLE AND ALTERNATIVE ENERGY USE AND ACHIEVE ENERGY INDEPENDENCE

Obama's plan to invest in a clean energy future and in renewable and alternative energies states that he will:[9]

INVEST $150 BILLION OVER TEN YEARS IN CLEAN ENERGY: Obama will invest $150 billion over ten years to advance the next generation of biofuels and fuel infrastructure, accelerate the commercialization of plug-in hybrids, promote development of commercial-scale renewable energy, invest in low-emissions coal plants, and begin the transition to a new digital electricity grid. . . .

DOUBLE ENERGY RESEARCH AND DEVELOPMENT FUNDING: Obama will double science and research funding for clean energy projects, including those that make use of our biomass, solar and wind resources.

INVEST IN A SKILLED CLEAN TECHNOLOGIES WORKFORCE: Obama will use proceeds from the cap and trade auction program to invest in job training and transition programs to help workers and industries adapt to clean technology development and production. Obama will also create an energy-focused Green Jobs Corps to connect disconnected and disadvantaged youth with job skills for a high-growth industry. . . .

DEVELOP AND DEPLOY CLEAN COAL TECHNOLOGY: Obama will significantly increase the resources devoted to the commercialization and deployment of low-carbon coal technologies. . . .

DEPLOY CELLULOSIC ETHANOL: Obama will invest federal resources, including tax incentives, cash prizes, and government contracts into developing the most promising technologies with the goal of getting the first two billion gallons of cellulosic ethanol into the system by 2013. . . .

INCREASE RENEWABLE FUEL STANDARD: Obama will require 36 billion gallons of renewable fuels to be included in the fuel supply by 2022 and will increase that to at least 60 billion gallons of advanced biofuels like cellulosic ethanol by 2030.

Obama intends to invest $150 billion over ten years to advance the next generation of biofuels and fueling station infrastructure.[10] At first blush, this certainly seems like a smart thing to do. Whatever we can do to reduce our dependence on foreign oil would have to be a good thing. But this plan also has its risks. The federal government is put in the position of having to determine which energy alternative, which biofuel, which electric or hydrogen fueled car should be the standard of the future and deserving of our subsidies. One could imagine the government subsidizing the creation of a national hydrogen car re-fueling network of service stations across the country only to find that hydrogen cars turn out to be impractical and do little to reduce carbon emissions. The federal government, with its lack of profit motive, may be a poor judge of the economic feasibility of alternative approaches to energy independence.

This is not a hypothetical situation. In the last year, the federal government has come out broadly in support of ethanol production from corn, and has granted enormous subsidies to corn growers. The price of corn has doubled, as farmers recognize that the government has anointed their product as the solution to our energy problems. Now, however, we are finding out that the production of ethanol from corn and its subsequent burning in an automobile's internal combustion engine creates more, not less, carbon dioxide, and more energy is required to grow and transport corn than it releases in combustion. The bottom line is that for every gallon of ethanol we produce, we make the global warming problem worse, not better. And from an ethical perspective, we have announced to the developing world that America would rather see a major food source like corn utilized to help drive Americans to the mall rather than feed the hungry of the planet. Many foodstuff prices have doubled in the last few years, causing a severe risk of starvation in the developing world, and the IMF has estimated at least half of this price increase is due to the advanced world's use of foodstuffs for energy uses like transportation.[11]

So, while Obama's intentions are good, it is very important that he exercise caution when applying subsidies and establishing infrastructure standards. The issue cannot be left to industry alone, which has dragged its feet in order to protect its oil revenues and its combustion engine car sales. But the government cannot become the sole decider of technological innovation. A reasonable approach would be for the government to fund smaller programs on a trial basis in cities and states across America and see which alternatives work best. While the impact of warming is global, the right approach to finding a solution should be local. Fleets of government vehicles can be converted to electricity or hydrogen in an attempt to see which is most cost efficient without building an entire network of electricity recharging stations across the country. Switch grass can be planted in Kansas and subsidies given to Kansas farmers to determine its potential as a bio-fuel without asking the entire world to adopt it as a winning alternative before the evidence is in. Obama will be wise to take small steps, initially, and to tread carefully so as not to send our country down a series of rather unproductive paths to energy independence.

Of course, from an economic perspective, the greatest motivation and incentive to develop alternative sources of energy, such as solar power, bio-fuels and wind power is to allow the market price of fossil fuels such as oil and gas to continue to increase. While citizens might complain about the higher cost of gasoline and heating oil, these higher energy prices are exactly the stimulus necessary to make solar power and wind power more competitive from a pricing standpoint. Simply stated, if oil prices ever went up to $200 per barrel, every roof in America would be covered with solar cells. While not the ideal solution, it does highlight the problem. We are not running out of energy, we are just running out of cheap energy.

One additional comment for Obama's consideration, with regard to the global price of oil, it is apparent that the supposedly "market" price of oil is anything but. Knowledgeable experts suggest that the current market price of oil should be more like $60 to $70 if supply and demand market forces controlled. The supply of oil on the market is determined by OPEC—a cartel, as in, a monopoly. The entire purpose of OPEC is to not allow the market price of oil to be achieved. OPEC arranges meetings whenever the price of oil begins to decline so they can adjust supply downward accordingly, and thus prevent any revenue loss. This violates the basic premise of free markets. One can argue whether there is anything we can do to prevent this monopolization of oil prices, but we should at least recognize that these OPEC countries are sticking it to us on very non-economic terms. President Bush saw fit to visit Saudi Arabia, and rather than deliver this tough economic message, found himself dancing in the streets with the kingdom's rulers. In addition, Bush entered into $20 billion of advanced arms sales to Saudi Arabia. Bush and his father have both benefited tremendously by Saudi Arabian investments in their private oil company enterprises and in their private equity funds over the years. One would hope that Obama would be much tougher on the Saudis and other OPEC members with regard to terms of trade, investing opportunities in the states, and weapons purchases, if they continue to push a monopolistic price of oil on the world.

People wonder why the United States is not building new refinery capacity. Some have argued that government regulation and environmentalists are to blame. The real reason is that the United States has burned through most of its oil reserves. You don't need refineries if you don't have oil in the ground. Many of our refineries were refining oil from the Middle East, but that flow has slowed tremendously as the Middle Eastern countries have decided to build their own refineries and process their own oil.

The key to energy independence and solving global warming is to make it a priority of the nation. Clearly, Barack Obama has this objective. But it is not enough to just talk about energy independence. The government must take action. No single oil company or electric utility acting to maximize their corporate profits would ever decide on their own to adopt energy independence as a national strategy. This is what governments are for, to identify national objectives, which may be outside the realm of the free markets, and establish cost-efficient systems to achieve them.

Obama's respect for the efficiency of the free market system will ensure that he does nothing to interfere with its operation. But he will not allow the free market for oil and electricity to proceed willy-nilly without a national objective of slowing global warming.

3. EMPHASIZE CONSERVATION AND IMPROVE ENERGY EFFICIENCY

Obama's plan states that it "will reduce oil consumption by at least 35 percent, or 10 million barrels per day, by 2030.[12] This will more than offset the equivalent of the oil we would import from OPEC nations in 2030." Obama's plan to set America on a path to energy independence states that he will:[13]

INCREASE FUEL ECONOMY STANDARDS: Obama will double fuel economy standards within eighteen years. His plan will provide retooling tax credits and loan guarantees for domestic auto plants and parts manufacturers, so that they can build new fuel efficient cars rather than overseas companies. Obama will also invest in advanced vehicle technology such as advanced lightweight materials and new engines.

SET NATIONAL BUILDING EFFICIENCY GOALS: Barack Obama will establish a goal of making all new buildings carbon neutral, or produce zero emissions, by 2030. He'll also establish a national goal of improving new building efficiency by 50 percent and existing building efficiency by 25 percent over the next decade to help us meet the 2030 goal.

INVEST IN A DIGITAL SMART GRID: Obama will pursue a major investment in our utility grid to enable a tremendous increase in renewable generation and accommodate modern energy requirements, such as reliability, smart metering, and distributed storage.

Though President Bush often stated that he is concerned about America's dependence on foreign oil, the one word that has never left his lips in eight years in office is "conservation." Conservation is a dirty word to Bush, who sees it as a threat to his energy company friends that people will be consuming less, not more, energy. Obama will make conservation a central tenet of his energy policies.[14] Obama has announced that he will double fuel economy standards within eighteen years, and that he will help domestic automobile manufacturers achieve these objectives by providing tax credits and loans guarantees for the required retooling.[15] Just because the federal government says something does not make it so. But in this case, a federal mandate to double fuel economy standards will indeed make it so. If the automakers cannot develop new engines and new technologies to achieve these results, they will, by mandate, just have to produce smaller cars with slightly worse acceleration. This is not the worst thing in the world. Someone today who wishes to buy a smaller, more fuel efficient car runs the risk of running into a Hummer on the highway, a difficult accident to survive. If all cars on the road weighed less, than it would be much less dangerous to drive a small car on our roads and highways.

Obama will establish a goal of making all new buildings carbon neutral by 2030.[16] He will establish a competitive grant program to reward those early adopters that will implement new building codes that emphasize energy efficiency.

As with all conservation, much of it begins at home. America is currently building new coal-fired power plants that are terrible carbon emitters in order to accomplish one goal of satisfying the peak energy needs of our electricity grid, a peak which occurs every day sometime between two to three o'clock in the afternoon, Eastern Standard Time. There is no shortage of electricity or energy on weekends, weekday mornings, or weekday evenings. Why? Because we charge the same amount for a kilowatt of electricity regardless of what time of day you consume it. Right now, there is no incentive for you not to turn on your dishwasher or your clothes dryer at 2:30 in the afternoon, even though by doing so you will be adding to an already overextended peak demand for electricity.

Obama would like to see a major investment in our utility grid and in smart electric metering in our homes and businesses, so that electricity consumed during peak hours will cost you more.[17] By putting a relatively inexpensive electronic chip in your thermostat you will be able to see the varying price of electricity during the day and make appropriate adjustments to your consumption. Already, entrepreneurs are developing smart thermostats that will communicate with your laptop computer and allow it to make adjustments to your thermostat settings based on the intraday prices of electricity. For example, if the peak price at 2:00 p.m. triples temporarily, your laptop computer, on its own, may decide to turn your air-conditioning down for a couple of hours in the afternoon.

4. REESTABLISH AMERICA AS THE GLOBAL LEADER IN GLOBAL WARMING NEGOTIATIONS[18]

Obama's plan to restore US leadership on climate change internationally states that he will:

CREATE NEW FORUM OF LARGEST GREENHOUSE GAS EMITTERS: Obama will create a Global Energy Forum—that includes all G-8 members plus Brazil, China, India, Mexico and South Africa—the largest energy consuming nations from both the developed and developing world . . .

RE-ENGAGE WITH THE UN FRAMEWORK CONVENTION ON CLIMATE CHANGE: The UNFCCC process is the main international forum dedicated to addressing the climate problem and an Obama administration will work constructively within it.[19]

While Obama has said that he wants America to take the lead in negotiating lower carbon dioxide emissions for all countries, it is not clear how that global cooperation would work. At an energy conference in New York in 2007,[20] a major energy investor gave a presentation in which he blamed China, India, and the rest of the developing world for the majority of the annual increase in global emissions of carbon dioxide. It is true that if you look solely at the increase in global carbon dioxide emissions each year, the developing world is responsible for a great majority of that increase. But in a world where the United States, on average, is emitting twenty to 200 times as much carbon dioxide per capita as countries of the developing world,[21] it seems crazy to say the developing world is at fault for this problem. One has to come at the problem, as Obama most likely will, with a basic understanding that all peoples of the world have the same rights to economic development, the same right of economic prosperity, and to the extent that any human has the right to pollute, it should be equal across all countries of the world, developing and advanced.

While this approach seems logical to most, it does have rather dire consequences. Given China and India's recent successes in economic development, there appears to be no reason why all the developing countries of the world will not eventually achieve a modern standard of living approximately equal to the United States. Given that the industrialized nations of the world represent only 15 percent of the population of the world and currently produce almost half of the worlds CO_2, such rapid economic development worldwide will be cataclysmic for global carbon dioxide production.[22]

If nothing is done to restrict carbon dioxide emissions, simple arithmetic suggests that one would expect per capita CO_2 levels to increase four-fold as the developing world catches up to our standard of living and level of production per capita. Under such a scenario, all the countries of the world could attempt to utilize modest carbon reducing strategies, and total carbon emissions would still increase dramatically.

This analysis indicates that the basic problem may not be industrial development and carbon emissions per capita, but rather, that there are just too many people on the planet. Another indicator that the planet may be overpopulated are the current water and energy shortages across countries of the world, which will only increase as the developing world advances. Water and energy consumption grow enormously through development. While he has not mentioned it as yet, Obama would be smart to reintroduce an emphasis on reducing the planet's population if he is looking for a longer term solution to the planet's clean energy needs.

Before Obama can make progress on reducing CO_2 emissions, which will involve some sacrifice on behalf of the American consumer, he best be sure that all Americans are on board with his objective. While most Americans recognize the threat of global warming, there are still some who are unconvinced that it is a real problem. This may be a result of the confusion planted by the corporate and energy lobby, which argues that global warming is not real and not a threat. Regardless, Obama should present his case to the public on why global warming presents such a threat to us and how certain the evidence is. It would not be productive to recreate the entire argument here that global warming is a real threat, but let us take a few minutes to examine the evidence and the argument, and to see if we can give Obama a leg up in his presentation to the American people.

From an ideological perspective, it is true that industry, especially carbon intensive industries like the power generation industry, have worked hard to muddle the debate on global warming. But it is also true that many who seek to restrict carbon emissions would not be sad if it meant slower global growth and a restriction on corporate power. It is difficult, with such an ideological divide, to have an honest presentation and debate of the facts, but let us try.

Whatever we say here will be a gross oversimplification, as the problem is enormously complex. In general, there are four building blocks to the "proof" that global warming caused by humans is real. First, there are extensive studies that demonstrate that carbon dioxide is a greenhouse gas. For example, laboratory studies show that greater CO_2 concentrations in the air do cause ambient air temperatures to rise. Second, there is sufficient evidence to claim that carbon dioxide levels in the atmosphere have been rising for the last hundred or so years. Third, global temperatures over the last hundred years appear to have increased approximately one degree celsius. And fourth, examining earth temperatures over hundreds of thousands of years seems to indicate a strong correlation between levels of CO_2 in the atmosphere and surface temperatures.

These four findings, in combination, appear to offer fairly convincing evidence that global warming is real, and that carbon dioxide concentrations in the atmosphere are the cause. If one believes that the reason for increased carbon dioxide concentrations in the atmosphere over the last hundred years is due to industrial development, with its increased burning of fossil fuels, than it is fairly easy to conclude that global warming is man-made. Not only did global warming appear as we entered the industrial age, but it now appears to be accelerating as large population centers like China, India and Brazil industrialize.

As always, one has to be careful to differentiate between correlations and causation. Just because carbon dioxide levels and temperatures have been increasing for the last hundred years does not mean necessarily that CO_2 levels are causing the temperature increase. It might be the case that the higher temperatures are in fact causing the higher CO_2 levels. Or possibly, an as yet unidentified third agent may be causing both to increase such that there is no real causality between carbon dioxide levels and temperature.

At this point, a reasonable person would have to be fairly convinced that man-made carbon dioxide emissions were causing an increase in global temperatures. But in the interest of full disclosure, there is one more relevant point that needs to be made about the evidence presented today. I don't believe you should get your scientific evidence from the movies, but in this case it is true that many Americans learned about the dangers of global warming from Al Gore's movie, *An Inconvenient Truth*.[23] While extremely well made and very educational, the movie made one important, and unfortunate, point. It has to do with the fourth leg of the "proof" listed above, which utilized ice core data to demonstrate a correlation between carbon dioxide levels and temperatures going back over one hundred and fifty thousand of years on this planet. Mr. Gore, in his movie, showed a dramatic timeline that demonstrated that whenever CO_2 levels went up, global temperatures went up, and when CO_2 levels went down, global temperatures went down. Gore mentions that there is some debate on these findings, but simplifies the issue to the audience by pointing at the strong correlation in his graph and indicating, "there must be something here."

Indeed, there is something here, but it is not necessarily the conclusion that Al Gore led the audience to make—mainly that higher CO_2 levels in history have produced higher global temperatures. A more detailed look at the data over the last 160,000 years shows that the global temperature increased first, followed by increased CO_2 concentrations in the atmosphere. The causality is backwards. Temperatures increase first, followed by carbon dioxide increases. It is now believed that this causality is just the opposite of what Mr. Gore attempted to present. It appears that as global temperatures fluctuate and rise, the oceans warm and release more CO_2 to the atmosphere, thus increasing CO_2 concentrations in the air.

The anti-global warming crowd might take information like this and run with it, arguing that the case for global warming has not been made with certainty. Michael Crichton, in his novel *State of Fear*,[24] argues that the evidence for global warming being real and caused by man is so weak as to not be able to be proved in a court of law. In a criminal court, the jury must be convinced beyond a reasonable doubt. No one has ever tried to quantify how certain a jury must be to reach this conclusion, but as we know, a very high threshold of certainty is required to prevent convicting an innocent man.

But this level of certainty should not be required in the global warming debate. While certainty is nice, much work in physics, mathematics and philosophy recently suggests that absolute certainty is an impossibility. So how certain do we have to be that global warming is real and caused by CO_2 emissions before we begin to act? What if, instead of global warming, we were talking about a very large asteroid that appeared to be heading on a direct path toward Earth? Let's assume scientists were only 10 percent certain that the asteroid would impact Earth. Let's also assume that we had the technology to protect ourselves from errant asteroids. Given the devastation that the asteroid would cause, and the fact that we had the wherewithal to protect ourselves, I think most of us would agree the certainty we have is sufficient to act.

So it is with global warming. We do not have to be 100 percent certain that it is real and caused by carbon dioxide emissions before we begin to act. It is in the nature of the global warming problem that nothing we can do today will solve the problem immediately. Therefore, given that almost all scientists and reasonable people believe there is a reasonable probability that carbon dioxide emissions by humans are causing global warming, it certainly appears that the time to act is now. Of course, if we are wrong, and if global temperatures continue to rise beyond our expectations as we cut our carbon emissions, or if we find another explanation for the global temperature increase, we can always stop our efforts to control carbon dioxide emissions and save any additional costs of the program.

A final argument of the anti-global warming crowd is that even if you assume carbon dioxide emissions by humans are causing a slight global temperature increase, it is rather insignificant, and any major disruptions to the Earth's ecology will occur over such a long period of time that humans will easily adapt. Even if temperatures rise, sea levels rise, and earth temperatures become more moderate, humans will adapt. We would expect a gradual slow migration north as countries like Canada achieve more moderate temperatures.

This seems to be an overly optimistic solution to the problem. If indeed humans are causing the temperature of the entire planet to increase one degree celsius every fifty to one hundred years, the planet is telling humans that development has gone too far, and changes need to be made. The earth's ecology is too delicately balanced to allow humans to exert such a large influence on the planet.

With Obama, for the first time in history, a United States president will introduce a detailed comprehensive plan to begin to deal with global warming.[25] Nothing can be done overnight to correct hundreds of years of neglect. But, for the first time, Obama will insist that America address global warming directly and reduce carbon emissions immediately, with a long-term goal of reducing all carbon emissions by 80 percent by the year 2050.[26] With Obama's emphasis on market-based solutions and on utilizing technological innovation to find a solution, global warming may not only be conquered, but at a cost that does not harm our country's economic prosperity or future growth.

Chapter Seven

AFFORDABLE HEALTHCARE

*. . . One of the proposals (to curtail lobbying) would
have ended the practice of letting senators fly on private jets at the cheaper first-class commercial rate . . .*

*It was the right thing to do, but I will not lie; the
first time I was scheduled for a four-city swing in two
days flying commercial, I felt some pangs of regret.
The traffic to O'Hare was terrible. When I got there
the flight to Memphis had been delayed. A kid spilled
orange juice on my shoe.*

*Then, while waiting in line, a man came up to
me, maybe in his mid-thirties, dressed in chinos and a
golf shirt, and told me that he hoped Congress would
do something about stem cell research this year. I have
early-stage Parkinson's disease, he said, and a son who
is three years old. I probably won't ever get to play
catch with him. I know it may be too late for me, but
there's no reason somebody else has to go through what
I'm going through.*

*These are the stories you miss, I thought to myself,
when you fly in a private jet.*[1]

It would be a good bet that less than one percent of Americans truly
understand the economics of our current healthcare system. Obama
has said that if we were starting over with a completely blank slate
he would favor the one-payer system that is used in almost every
developed country in the world. But we aren't starting from scratch.

The problem is enormously complex. In this case complexity has
benefited the healthcare providers and has effectively kept the pub-

lic out of the debate, because so few understand the issues. It has allowed crazy pricing, because with so many products and services it is difficult to make comparisons across providers. And it has minimized regulation, because the regulators just can't keep up with the innovation and complexity.

Obama recognizes that 47 million Americans, including nearly 9 million children are not covered by health insurance.[2] Obama's plan is to create a health insurance system that will cover all Americans, including the self-employed and small businesses. Under his plan, nobody will be turned down from insurance because of pre-existing conditions. All essential medical services will be covered, including mental healthcare. An emphasis will be placed on funding preventative health expenditures, as currently they encompass only 4 percent of healthcare spending, yet provide a great opportunity to reduce healthcare expenses over the long run. Obama promises that the new plan will be portable; a person will be able to move from job to job without having to change his coverage. From his healthcare position paper entitled, "Plan for a Healthy America," I quote:

OBAMA'S PLAN TO COVER UNINSURED AMERICANS: Obama will make available a new national health plan to all Americans, including the self-employed and small businesses, to buy affordable health coverage that is similar to the plan available to members of Congress. . . . Obama will require that all children have healthcare coverage.

REDUCING COSTS OF CATASTROPHIC ILLNESSES FOR EMPLOYERS AND THEIR EMPLOYEES: The Obama plan would reimburse employer health plans for a portion of the catastrophic costs they incur . . .

HELPING PATIENTS: Support disease management programs. Coordinate and integrate care. Require full transparency about quality and costs.

ENSURING PROVIDERS DELIVER QUALITY CARE: Promote patient safety. Align incentives for excellence. Tackle disparities in healthcare. Insurance reform . . .

LOWERING COSTS THROUGH INVESTMENT IN ELECTRONIC HEALTH INFORMATION TECHNOLOGY SYSTEMS: Obama will invest $10 billion a year over the next five years to move the US healthcare system to broad adoption of standards-based electronic health information systems.

LOWERING COSTS BY INCREASING COMPETITION IN THE INSURANCE AND DRUG MARKETS: Barack Obama will prevent companies from abusing their monopoly power through unjustified price increases.

LOWER PRESCRIPTION DRUG COSTS: Obama will allow Americans to buy their medicines from other developed countries if the drugs are safe and prices are lower outside the US Obama will also repeal the ban that prevents the government from negotiating with drug companies, which could result in savings as high as $30 billion. Finally, Obama will work to increase the use of generic drugs . . .

IMPROVE MENTAL HEALTHCARE: Mental illness affects approximately one in five American families. . . . As president, Obama will support mental health parity so that coverage for serious mental illnesses are provided on the same terms and conditions as other illnesses and diseases.[3]

Obama expects that the premiums paid by most Americans will decline and subsidies will be offered to more moderate-income people to allow them to buy into the plan. Of course, this is not all free. Obama's team estimates they it should cost approximately $100 billion a year. Obama does not intend to raise average Amercians' taxes to pay for the plan, but rather intends to fund the plan from the government savings he expects we will get by pulling our troops out of Iraq and ending the war, from the tax increase he proposes for Americans earning over $250,000 per year, and from the money he raises by instituting a carbon tax on carbon dioxide emissions. In addition, Obama will mandate that employers who are not currently paying for quality healthcare coverage for their employees will have to contribute a percentage of their payroll costs to the plan.[4]

By introducing a plan to insure that almost all Americans will have adequate health insurance, Obama will also be benefitting the hospitals who have provided last resort medical care to the poor and indigent. Emergency rooms across the country are full of people without insurance who have no family practitioner, and who utilize the emergency room for almost all of their medical care. With no one left to bill, hospitals often provide emergency room services to the uninsured for non-life-threatening care, either free or at substantially reduced cost. Emergency room care is some of the most expensive care in a hospital and is a large loss leader for a hospital, given that it is currently subsidizing the uninsured. Hospitals would save something on the order of $10 to $50 billion a year if they did not have to provide this free medical care to the uninsured.[5] Obama should think of a way to capture some of the savings that the hospitals will gain. One can argue that is not right that hospitals have to pay for medical care for the uninsured, but again, that is the current situation, and they should be amenable to paying something to have this cost burden removed from their books.

Obama's plan is strong on reducing costs. Seventy-five percent of all healthcare expenditures are for patients with chronic conditions such as heart disease and diabetes. Obama will require that providers utilize proven disease management programs for these chronic conditions. One hundred and thirty-three million Americans have at least one chronic disease, and the cost is a staggering

$1.7 trillion annually.[6] Because exercise is so important to keep weight off and staying healthy, Obama would be smart to find some way to get Americans out of their cars, away from their televisions, and out walking and running again.

Just as Obama plans to increase transparency in Washington to implement lobbyist reform, transparency will help him to improve medical quality and control costs. He will require hospitals to publicly report detailed information on their cost and quality of care, including data on medical errors, nurse staffing ratios, hospital acquired infections, and so on. Health plans will be required to disclose the percentage of premiums that go to patient care as opposed to administrative costs. Obama will further lower costs by moving medical records online. He will spend $10 billion a year over the next five years to create an electronic health information system that will move patients records online and that will ensure patient's privacy is protected.[7]

Obama seeks to lower costs further by increasing competition in the medical insurance and pharmaceutical industries. The insurance business today is dominated by a small group of very large companies. The two largest health insurance companies represent more than a 33 percent market share. Obama seeks to control unjustified price increases by medical insurance companies, and will force insurers to pay a significant percentage of premiums toward patient care rather than to overhead costs and shareholder dividends and repurchase programs.[8]

Obama recognizes that Europe and Canada are selling the exact same drugs available here at half the price. Obama will allow Americans to buy their medicines internationally in an effort to break up this geographic monopoly. Obama will also repeal the ban that prevents our government from negotiating with drug companies on the prices they charge Medicare and Medicaid, which may result in savings as high as $30 billion. And Obama will see that Medicare, Medicaid, and other governmental programs make full use of lower-cost generic drugs.[9]

Obama must take care not to accept the current artificially high prices charged by medical practitioners and drug companies as the norm. Although he is coming into the game in the seventh inning, it is important that he does more than just build a generous reimbursement system that funds the current high price environment. In order to be successful, he must figure out a way to reduce the number of medical procedures, the drugs consumed, and to reduce the prices paid. If all he does is increase taxes to pay for an expensive and rapidly growing healthcare system, it will be a failure.

Although he has not mentioned it in his campaign, and there is no reason to think he is even thinking about it, Obama and Congress could make a simple change that would alter the dynamics of pricing in the drug industry overnight. If the drug lobbyists were overruled and shorter patent lives were given to new drugs the wait for generics to appear in the market would be much shorter. Yes, shorter patent lives means fewer dollars dedicated to research of new drugs, but isn't that just what we want? Aren't we saying that we are spending too much time and effort finding new drugs that are so expensive they can only be afforded by a few? It would be better to shorten patent lives and get companies more focused on finding cures for ailments that afflict us all, rather than high-priced drugs available only to the rich that are bankrupting our healthcare system.

Healthcare spending currently represents 16 percent of the entire GDP and by 2016 it is expected to represent approximately 20 percent of our GDP.[10] The healthcare system is notoriously inefficient and there are savings to be had by reducing paperwork, streamlining procedures, eliminating bureaucracy and redundancy, and moving more patient information online where it will be portable and accessible, as Obama suggests in his policy statements.

But if we solely focus our efforts on improving efficiency and cost reductions, we will not get to the real problem in our healthcare system. Yes, we would have savings, but instead of 20 percent of our GDP going to healthcare in eight years, the percentage may drop to something like 18 percent. Even at this level, healthcare expenditures would still be a significant drain on the productive capacity of Americans, and we would have done little to slow its growth in the future.

Inefficiencies in the system are a problem, but the real reason that healthcare costs are exploding as a percentage of GDP in America is that Americans are consuming many more pharmaceuticals than they have in the past, undergoing many more medical procedures than before, and paying a much bigger price for both. The quantity of healthcare consumed per person is exploding, and the pricing of that healthcare is also rapidly increasing. If the amount you buy of something increases rapidly, and the price you pay is also increasing, you need only multiply these two figures to see why the total cost of the product or service is rapidly expanding. Economics suggests we might want to buy less of an item as its price increases. Healthcare seems to violate that basic fundamental principle of economics.

To oversimplify—because that is what is needed to see the big picture problem in healthcare—there are two basic ways countries provide healthcare to their citizens. Most of the advanced countries of the world utilize a one-payer system, in which employees and employers contribute premiums to the government, and the government pays all medical expenses for its citizens. The alternative is to have a system that depends primarily on private insurance, in which the government stays out of it, pharmaceuticals and medical procedures are offered on a market basis just like any other product or service, and consumers enter into agreements with private insurance companies that allow individuals to pay regular insurance premiums and receive healthcare in return.

Of course, there are problems with both. Under a one-payer system, the government runs the healthcare system, and so you would come to expect the inefficiencies, bureaucracy, and waiting in lines typically associated with government-run programs. Because there is little competition under a one-payer system, you run the risk of creating a system that does not provide the services desired by the public. Entrepreneurship, innovation, new technology, and new product introduction is not discouraged by the system, but neither can we say it is encouraged.

Under a purely private insurance system, something along the lines of how health insurance is provided to the wealthier in America, you would expect better efficiencies and greater innovation, as it should be more competitive and more market oriented. There are problems. Medical procedures and pharmaceuticals will be developed that not all can afford. The wealthy will buy high premium gold-plated plans that cover any medical expense required in their lifetime, but the middle class and the poor will not be able to afford to participate in such plans. If poor and moderate income people choose not to purchase insurance, society has to decide how much medical care to provide them when they become sick.

The United States currently is stuck somewhere in between these two alternatives. Some would argue that rather than grabbing the best from each, America has grabbed the worst. Our system has all the inefficiency of the government-run program, but all of the freedom to raise prices as in the market-driven private insurance plan.

While Obama has said that if he could start over he would favor a one-payer system, he recognizes that it is almost impossible to forget history.[11] One lesson that Obama writes about in his books is that history is always with us. Obama has led his life in search of his own personal history and his family's, because he is a believer that history is a prime determinant of who we are.[12] Obama, a realist, believes that in addressing a problem you cannot apply a theoretical ideal developed in the laboratory; you must start with the system's current situation and try to make incremental progress. His community organizing work has taught him the realities of power-based negotiation, in which the status quo is always supported by strong and vocal forces that must be overcome to accomplish change. To assume these sources of entrenched power will just disappear and let you do what you want is naïve.

Obama is not going to implement a one-payer system. He is going to work with the existing system and try to tweak it so that it provides healthcare to all Americans at a more reasonable cost. Obama likes the idea of utilizing market-based forces to accomplish such objectives, but would never go so far as to allow market oriented forces to prevent all Americans from receiving healthcare.

One of Obama's principal advisers on healthcare is David Cutler.[13] He is an economist who has written extensively on the problems in the healthcare system. He is most noted for suggesting that it is not a problem that Americans pay 16 percent of GDP on healthcare. Like most market-based economists, he argues that if Americans are paying for it, they must see value in the healthcare services they are buying, and so, by definition, it's not a problem. Who are we to say that Americans are consuming too much healthcare? Let the market decide, and let Americans decide how much of their money they wish to spend on healthcare versus other products and services such as housing, food, apparel, automotives, vacations, and so on.[14]

Such an approach works for a more standard market provided commodity. Healthcare is unique in a number of aspects. First, society seems to believe that all people deserve some level of healthcare. If a market-oriented healthcare approach resulted in 10 to 15 percent of Americans not being covered, this would be unacceptable to most Americans.

Second, healthcare insurance is a very long-lived asset, like other insurance products, savings and investment products, and houses and home mortgages that the free market historically has done a poor job of pricing properly. Many people just don't seem to have a long enough consumption/investment time horizon to make intelligent choices about paying a healthcare premium today to secure healthcare benefits when they are older. An eighty-year-old would be willing to pay for a procedure that adds five years to his life, but a thirty-year-old wouldn't necessarily pay a higher premium now to live to eighty-five rather than eighty.

Finally, healthcare is a difficult product to create an active market for. People like seeing and trusting one physician, but by doing so, in effect, they have created a monopoly provider for medical services. All healthcare consumption, even medical procedures performed by specialists, flows through this single distribution channel. It is difficult to create a true market of many buyers and sellers under such constraints.

This can be demonstrated with an example. Lasix surgery to correct vision problems used to be a procedure that was not paid for by most medical insurance plans. Technically, it was a procedure that fell outside the traditional services that a general practitioner might perform or recommend. A healthy market-based system developed that encouraged innovation, competition, cost savings, and price reductions. What was once a procedure only available to higher-income people with a cost of over $10,000 can now be accomplished for under $2,000.

If we wanted to move to a more market-based system of providing healthcare, this is what the world would look like. Multiple providers, less allegiance to your family physician, much more advertising and promotion, and more deceptive pricing and promotion gimmicks, but in the long run, probably less expensive healthcare.

Most healthcare expenditures occur at the end of one's life. If recent studies on Medicare expenditures are to be believed, as much as 30 percent of the total healthcare expenditures you'll make in your lifetime will occur in the last year of your life, with a great proportion of those occurring in the last two weeks of your life. If you want to rein in healthcare costs, it seems logical that this is a good place to start.

Although he has not said anything about it yet in his campaign, for obvious political reasons, Obama would be wise once he is in office to think of ways of reducing this enormous cost on society. It's not as if we can continue to make this level of commitment to our seniors. It is currently being funded by the younger generation in one of the most unjust financing schemes of all time; they pay for their grandparents' care, but there are not enough dollars in the system to pay for their own care when they become older.

One of the ways to get these late-in-life medical costs under control is to encourage living wills that make greater use of hospice providers. Without a living will, medical practitioners, sworn to the Hippocratic oath, spend enormous sums of money keeping the dying alive for one more day. Often, the elderly person suffers from senility, Alzheimer's, or other mental impairments, causing him to be completely unaware of his circumstances and unappreciative of the effort being made to prolong his life.

Another, much larger, reform to the healthcare system that Obama may wish to consider is to develop a two-tier system of medical insurance. You can't wait until someone is eighty years old to ask them if they would like the most expensive medical care and procedures necessary to prolong their life. All of them would want it. The choice should be given to the eighty-year-old, but at a much younger time in his life. A twenty-five-year-old, starting his business career, could be given the choice between two different medical insurance plans. One would have a very high monthly premium and provide the best medical care possible throughout his lifetime. The second plan would provide the best medical care possible until the age of seventy-five, at which point, if the person became life-threateningly ill, and the doctors felt it was appropriate, they could move him into a hospice situation, in which some overly expensive procedures might be denied. The quid pro quo, and the reason why a young person may sign on to such a plan, is that it would have dramatically lower monthly premiums associated with it, possibly less than half of the alternative cradle-to-grave premium plan. Now, when it comes time to decide which eighty-year-old receives the expensive care to prolong his life by an additional two weeks and which eighty-year-old will be moved into hospice, the decision will have already been made. And the beauty of this plan is that the decision will have been made by the individual himself at a time in his life when he was fully rational, when he was young. In addition, he will have received the benefit of much lower insurance premiums for his entire life in exchange for such an agreement, so the plan passes the fairness test. One can imagine some difficulty in enforcing such contracts, but if we are to contain the rapidly escalating expense of caring for our seniors, such a plan might be attractive, especially to our young people who are paying for all this.

So Obama promotes a system that is a marriage of the two extremes, an expanded Medicare and Medicaid system for the elderly, poor, and moderate income people, and a private insurance system for the more well off.[15] Unlike President Bush's attempt to provide pharmaceutical coverage for seniors, which did nothing more than preserve a high-cost drug pricing system paid for on the back of younger taxpayers, Obama's changes will attempt to lower costs by making the system more transparent and more competitive. To be effective, Obama will have to take on the pharmaceutical, HMO, physician and hospital lobbies. They will not be in favor of cutting prices and increasing competition, or of making their plans more understandable by making them more transparent.

Regardless of whether his proposals are paid for in advance through tax increases and other government expenditure cutbacks, it would be imprudent to continue to spend as much as we are on healthcare. We got into this predicament by allowing the number of procedures, the amount of pharmaceuticals, and the prices to increase on an uncontrolled basis for decades. To fund this high level of expenditure through taxpayer expense would be a shame. To find the real solution to the healthcare dilemma, Obama should pretend that we only have 10 percent of GDP available to spend on healthcare, not 16 percent, and then ask the tough question on how we contain costs at that level. He will conclude that efficiency savings through automation and the elimination of bureaucratic and redundant procedures will not be sufficient. A bold initiative must be undertaken to reduce the quantity of healthcare services and pharmaceuticals consumed by the chronically ill, the dying, and those living unhealthy lifestyles. Smart care can be provided on an affordable basis such that all can be cared for at a much lower cost to society.

Just as Obama is planning an 80 percent reduction target for carbon dioxide emissions by 2050, he would be wise to rein in many other problems facing America, rather than just funding them at the current level. Healthcare should not be funded at 16 percent of GDP; rather, plans should be made to see if its total cost can be lowered to 10 percent of GDP. We should not pay interest on $10 trillion of debt forever; instead, we should see if we can pay back and halve our debt somehow. Current levels of social security and Medicare spending should not be financed; we should find a way to reduce this burden on future generations. The military should not be funded at the current inflated $800 billion level, but rather at half that level. If Obama enacted such a fiscally responsible plan, government spending would be reduced, budgets would be balanced, and more resources would be available for private sector growth and development. Obama will fall short of his vision of creating a vibrant and growing economy if all that he does is fund current levels of healthcare and government spending at their already outrageous levels.

Chapter Eight

THE AGING OF THE POPULATION

What would the Ownership Society do with the losers (if Social Security were privatized)? Unless we're willing to see seniors starve on the street, we're going to have to cover their retirement expenses one way or another—and since we don't know in advance which of us will be losers, it makes sense for all of us to chip into a pool that gives us at least some guaranteed income in our golden years. That doesn't mean we shouldn't encourage individuals to pursue higher-risk, higher-return investment strategies. They should. It just means that they should do so with savings other than those put into Social Security.[1]

Thus, Obama was able to cut through all the rhetoric and see the key underlying fallacy of Bush's and McCain's proposal to privatize Social Security. If we allow people to invest in riskier assets in the stock market, we will just have more losers who end up gambling with their retirement money and end up with nothing at retirement and under Bush's plan, with no one to care for them. This is an example of Obama's greatest strength, the wisdom to see the underlying fundamental causes of our problems, so that we might structure real solutions that will be effective.

The eldest of the post-war baby boomers are now sixty-two years old and rapidly approaching retirement age. Much has been said about the effects of aging on the health of the nation's retirement system, but the effects could be much more pervasive and dramatically affect economies around the world. Larry Kotlikoff of Boston University has written a book entitled *The Coming Generational Storm*[2] in which he shows that income taxes would have to be raised by 60 percent immediately to make the cost of Social Security and Medicare fall more equally on different generations.

Obama is committed to ensuring Social Security is solvent and viable for the American people. Taken directly from his policy paper on the subject, below are some quoted excerpts of steps Obama would take to ensure that our elderly are properly cared for.

PAYROLL TAXES: Obama believes that the first place to look for ways to strengthen Social Security is the payroll tax system. Currently, the Social Security payroll tax applies to only the first $97,500 a worker makes. Obama supports increasing the maximum amount of earnings covered by Social Security and he will work with Congress and the American people to choose a payroll tax reform package that will keep Social Security solvent for at least the next half century.

REFORM CORPORATE BANKRUPTCY LAWS TO PROTECT WORKERS AND RETIREES: Current bankruptcy laws protect banks before workers. Obama will protect pensions by putting promises to workers higher on the list of debts that companies cannot shed.

ELIMINATE INCOME TAXES FOR SENIORS MAKING LESS THAN $50,000: Obama will eliminate all income taxation of seniors making less than $50,000 per year.

PROVIDE CHEAPER PRESCRIPTION DRUGS: Our seniors pay the highest prices in the world for brand-name drugs. To lower drug costs, Obama will allow the federal government to negotiate for lower drug prices for the Medicare program, just as it does to lower prices for our veterans.

PROTECT AND STRENGTHEN MEDICARE: Obama is committed to the long-term strength of the Medicare program. He will reduce waste in the Medicare system, including eliminating subsidies to the private insurance Medicare Advantage program.

Let us examine in much deeper detail some of these proposals, especially those regarding how Social Security will be funded going forward.

Conservatives in America admit there is a serious problem with the future funding of Social Security and Medicare, but downplay its importance by suggesting there is a readily available solution that can correct any shortfall. Their proposed solution is to partially privatize Social Security by allowing individuals to opt out of Social Security and instead manage their own private retirement accounts. The thought is that individuals would invest more heavily in the stock market, and could generate substantial enough returns to offset any shortfalls resulting from the Social Security plan. Obama is strongly against such a plan.

This proposal to privatize social security is flawed in a number of very important aspects. First, there is no money in the Social Security system to invest. It is a pay-as-you go system—current workers are funding current retirees, and must look to future generations to fund their own retirement expenses.

Second, just because common equities have outperformed US Treasuries historically does not mean that they will in the future. The reason they have yielded more on average historically is that they are riskier—in other words, more volatile—and the US economy has done very well over the last one hundred years. There is no guarantee that the US will be the dominant economic power in the world in the next century—just ask China and India—and so there is no guarantee that US equities will outperform fixed income investments going forward.

Some people mistakenly think that the volatility issue is not a concern if equities are held for a long enough period. There is no holding period, even of fifty years or more, at which one can be certain that equities will outperform bonds or even that their total return will be positive. It is hard for Americans to see this, given how successful their equity market has been historically, but it is much easier to see if one thinks about investing in a country such as Germany or Japan. There is no guarantee that the equity markets of those countries will outperform their sovereign debt in the long term.

Which brings us to the third fallacy of the privatization approach. Individuals can invest their own savings any way they want, because society doesn't suffer if they win or lose in their investment strategy. But if an individual wishes to exempt himself from Social Security, manage his own retirement funds, and invest aggressively in risky equities, who has to pick up the bill when he has no funds available for retirement? The taxpayer. As Obama says, society is not going to let the elderly starve in retirement, regardless of how unsuccessful they turn out to be as investors.[3] Therefore, it makes little sense to allow individuals to pursue their own risky investment strategies, and it also makes little sense to invest any Social Security surpluses in the stock market. They should be invested right where they are funding current retirees and in safe Treasury securities. If individuals wish to pursue riskier strategies with their overall portfolio, they are welcome to do so with their private investments, knowing that their minimum retirement needs are invested conservatively.

Critics argue that Social Security and Medicare are more than $50 trillion in deficit over their life.[4] This is a staggering number equal to more than three times the size of America's total GDP.

Some argue that Social Security has performed wonderfully to date and is fully funded for at least another forty years, and that the only way for critics to project such large shortfalls in the future is to assume only 1.5 percent growth rates for the US economy, far below its historical growth rate.

While such low projected growth rates seem conservative, one must remember they are real growth rates that ignore the effects of inflation. Also, they are per capita growth rates that would be adjusted upward if America's population continued to increase in the future. For example, if America's population increased at 1.5 percent per year and it had inflation of 4 percent per year, one would need nominal growth of 7 percent per year to achieve 1.5 percent real per capita growth. We shall see that even 1.5 percent real per capita growth in the economy might be difficult to achieve in the future as a major demographic shift occurs in America.

Obama recognizes that Medicare faces funding issues in the next twenty to thirty years and that we must do something to provide a more secure foundation to its programs. But Obama has been more vocal in arguing that Social Security is in a much better position, financially speaking, than Medicare. Obama's plan is to protect social security benefits for both current and future beneficiaries. He does not believe it is necessary to raise the retirement age in order to do this. And, as mentioned previously, he is strongly opposed to privatizing Social Security.[5]

To pay for shortfalls in the Social Security system, Obama would like to see the payroll tax threshold raised. Currently an employee and employer only pay Social Security tax on the first $97,500 a worker makes. Obama would like to see this threshold raised. In effect, this increases the percentage of the Social Security costs that wealthier Americans would have to pay.

Given all the windfalls that the Bush administration has provided the wealthy in this country, it is difficult to argue that such a plan to more heavily tax the wealthy is unfair. But, in combination with Obama's plan to terminate the Bush tax cuts for the wealthiest Americans and return their income tax rates to 39 percent, it is true that the wealthy will be paying a significant percentage of their income in taxes. Under Obama's plan, the wealthy would end up paying 39 percent in income tax, 12 percent in payroll taxes for Social Security, and another 6 to 10 percent in local income taxes. This means, in aggregate, wealthy Americans would be paying approximately 60 percent of their income in taxes to the government. Combine this with 6 to 8.5 percent sales taxes, local property taxes, and capital gain taxes, and some will be paying close to 70 percent of their income each year in taxes.

If 60 percent to 70 percent of our country's wealthiest citizens' incomes are going to the government, it suggests that we are rapidly approaching the limits of what our citizens can pay in aggregate to finance this government. This suggests that Obama would be wise to not only support government programs that are budget neutral because they have been paid for, but also look to find ways to reduce the overall size of government and its burden on American citizens. Social Security and Medicare are a substantial portion of all government spending, so it would be wise to examine ways to bring their costs under control.

Rather than completely funding the current Social Security plan as originally structured, Obama could propose changes in the system that will lower its overall cost and thus reduce the tax burden for all Americans. One such idea that Obama may choose to consider is to make Social Security much more of an insurance program against elderly poverty than a guaranteed income stream for all seniors. Theoretically, you could structure Social Security as a system into which everybody makes a lower premium payment, but out of which only people who are truly needy ever take money. or example, if seniors have other income besides Social Security from part-time jobs, dividend income, tax-free bonds, and other savings, or if their wealth is so substantial that they can live off of it without additional inflows of cash, then they might agree to return a portion of their Social Security payments. The savings would ensure a dramatically lower cost to the system, lower premiums paid by the younger generation, and a Social Security system resting on a much firmer foundation. You could even guarantee a senior that if he spent his life savings over a longer than expected retirement—in effect, if he outlived his savings—Social Security would be there to make sure he didn't suffer.

Another action that Obama might want to consider, and that has not been mentioned anywhere as yet, would be to claw back some of the Social Security benefits paid to the better off recipients from their surviving estates after their deaths. The elderly probably would not support a reduction in their annual Social Security payments, because they do not know how long they will live and what medical care they will require. But they may be much more amenable to giving something back to the system once they have died.

Times have dramatically changed since the Social Security system was enacted by Roosevelt in 1934. At that time, it was very true that a great majority of the elderly were living in poverty. Social Security was initially intended as an insurance program to guarantee that if you worked productively your entire life you would never have to live your retirement years in poverty.

Two things changed over time. First, Social Security has become more of an entitlement to all elders, not just those living in poverty. And, more importantly, due to a number of factors, the elderly in America are much better off financially. Americans over sixty-five years of age have a median wealth per person of approximately $230,000, and it is increasing each year. (Isn't wealth supposed to decline in retirement as you consume it to pay for retirement?) This compares with median wealth per person of $70,000 for those aged thirty-five to forty-four, and only $14,000 for adults aged eighteen to thirty-five.[6] This wealth for the elderly generates tremendous dividend, interest, and capital gains income, which could provide ample earnings for the retired to live on. In addition, many elderly have fairly generous defined-benefit pension plans from their employers or from the government, something most younger Americans do not have. Seventy-five percent of the elderly in America over the age of sixty-five own their own homes outright with no mortgage, so they face no monthly mortgage payment.[7] In essence, we are asking our youngest Americans to forgo 12 percent of their paychecks to fund the living expenses of their grandparents, who are much better off financially than they are themselves.

Even if a retired senior had no pension and no current income, life cycle theories of investing assume that the retired person will save during his productive working years and then watch that savings decrease as he consumes his savings in order to pay for living expenses in retirement. Very few seniors in this country are actually seeing a decline of their savings in order to fund their retirements.[8] To make the entire system more fair across the generations, these Social Security payments to the elderly could be means tested, not only for earnings, but also for wealth. Social Security would only be paid to those who need it to stay out of poverty, turning the system from an annuity into a true poverty insurance program, and thus dramatically lowering the cost and the premium burden on the younger generation.

Think about it in aggregate. Over $1/2 trillion in benefits each year is being paid out to the elder generation through Social Security.[9] An additional $1/2 trillion is going to the same group through medical care provided by Medicare and Medicaid.[10] These are direct transfers from the younger generation to the elder. In addition, from a cash flow perspective, Americans over sixty-five earn approximately $1 trillion in dividend, interest income and capital gains. In effect, Americans under forty who hold less than 5 percent of all the wealth in America are paying $2 trillion a year to Americans over sixty-five years old, who hold 85 percent of our wealth. It does not seem unreasonable to ask seniors to pay a greater percentage of their retirement costs, especially given that their medical care is provided for and most of their homes have already been paid for. It's hard to imagine where a senior living in rural America spends $25,000 in Social Security benefits, given that his children are grown, he has already paid for their education, his house mortgage is paid off, and his medical care is free. $25,000 a year buys a whole lot of dental floss and bingo cards.

We can hope that, once in office, President Obama has the foresight to pursue even more aggressive reform of the Social Security system then he suggested in his campaign. Is there a funding problem with Social Security and Medicare or not? It turns out that the problem is so big that the privatization scheme suggested by the conservatives will do little to prevent it. The liberals were wrong to downplay the enormity of the problem, and the conservatives are wrong to suggest they have a relatively easy and painless cure involving privatization.

First, today in America, there are only three workers for every retiree. This compares with over thirty workers for every retiree back in the 1940s, and less than two workers for every retiree once the baby boomers retire. This is a critical ratio to determine the health and viability of the Social Security systems, because current workers are funding the expenses of current retirees. Elderly Americans who claim they are due their retirement payments because they funded them their whole lives are mistaken. They funded past retirees, who numbered far fewer, lived shorter lives, and spent much less on healthcare expenditures. The only reason the current system is still solvent today is that current retirees have the baby boom behind them, a large, very productive workforce that is working like crazy and getting taxed like crazy to pay for the recent expensive medical miracles that keep current retirees alive. Shortly after the baby boom fully retires, there will not be enough highly productive, highly paid workers to pay for the large number of retirees in the future.

People used to work from age sixteen (twelve on the farm) until at least sixty-five. Typically, they would work for fifty years, annually contributing into Social Security, and then retire for ten or fifteen years till their death in their sixties or seventies. Today, with kids spending more time in college and graduate schools and people retiring earlier, it is not atypical for someone to work from ages twenty-five to sixty, and then retire early. With dramatically increased life expectancy today, this can mean an individual might work for thirty-five years, and retire for thirty or more golden years. There is no national retirement investment plan that can support that kind of life plan. Again, the only reason the numbers have not exploded already is that the current hardworking and large baby boom is funding the spending excesses of today's less numerous elderly.

The funding problem is compounded by the fact that many people are living beyond eighty-five years old. The US Census bureau estimates the number of elderly Americans eighty-five years old and over will increase from approximately 5 million today to close to 20 million persons by the year 2040.[11] This is an extremely important group to watch, as they have the greatest needs for medical, institutionalized, and home healthcare. Advanced science is keeping us alive longer, but is not suggesting how society should pay for the care of the elderly that is required.

The other reason that Social Security has remained viable to date is that the payroll tax used to fund it has grown steadily over the years. The statutory rate is now 12 percent, if both employee and employer contributions are included. This is the most regressive of taxes, as it applies only to the first $97,500 dollars earned and so the working poor and middle class are hit the hardest as a percentage of total earnings. There is a very good argument that such a high payroll tax is already interfering with the ability of our working poor to pay for necessities like adequate food, shelter, and healthcare, and may be causing a negative impact on economic growth in America. Economists estimate that the payroll tax will have to double in the future in order to fund the shortfalls in Social Security and Medicare. Such an increase would be devastating for the working poor and the middle-income people, and would have an immediate and permanent impact on the future growth of America's economy.

Many analyses of the aging problem in the United States focus on the demographic population bubble created by the baby boom. Little detailed work is done beyond a general recognition that there is a large number of people expected to retire in the very near future. But focusing solely on population statistics only tells a portion of the story. To understand how dramatic an event the baby boomers retiring will be, one has to examine the earnings power of that generation as compared to future generations. The proper analysis is not concerned with the number of people who are retiring, but their earnings power. That is what has to be replaced to keep GDP growing and to maintain a strong tax base in order to fund Social Security and Medicare in the future.

When one looks beyond population statistics and begins to examine lost earnings potential, the story becomes even more grim. The baby boomers, regardless of their faults, are extremely hardworking and very productive. America is at its peak international political and economic power. It is hard to imagine it being able to extract more value from its trading partners than it is doing today. An optimist might argue that technology and computers will dramatically increase productivity in the future, and this is partly true. But, to the extent the next generation after the baby boomers utilize their technological superiority to solely advance their entertainment needs—more narly video games, better music delivery, bigger televisions—the overall impact on future economic growth will be limited.

What all analyses of the problem have ignored to date is that many of the young people coming after the baby boom are not as well prepared to contribute to a globally competitive economy. Americans have less of an aging demographic population bulge problem than many European countries, but that is because they have had much greater immigration. Some of this immigration represents foreign students who attend US universities and then decide to stay, but the vast majority of immigrants are poor and come to the US seeking a better life for their families. If GDP is impacted negatively, the results will be devastating. First, any sort of solvency for Social Security and Medicare assumes fairly good growth rates in GDP. In essence, optimists hope, a la supply side economics, that funding shortfalls in the system will be taken care of by greater economic growth. If that growth does not materialize, the solvency of Social Security and Medicare will be at risk. Second, as growth stalls, taxes will have to be raised to pay for the retirement system, and such taxes will have an even greater negative impact on growth. And finally—and this is what no one has focused on yet—we may not have just a Social Security funding problem but a contracting economy problem.

Think of the baby boom workers as a group who will one day come in and inform their bosses they are done, they are quitting. The natural presumption is that you can just go out and hire some young gun to replace them. But there are two problems with that assumption. First, there aren't enough post boomers available to replace them all. And secondly, the labor pool that will be available after the baby boomers check out has much less experience in business, and cannot be expected to be nearly as productive.

At the same time, the boomers themselves will see their earning power drop dramatically as they enter retirement, and they will adjust their consumption down accordingly. Their never-ending thirst for greater and greater material consumption, while not the perfect formula for inner peace, will be missed greatly by the economy as a whole.

The problem is exacerbated by international trade with extremely poor countries such as China and India. Such trade puts additional wage pressure on the working poor and middle class— exactly the group we are hoping will bail us out of our retirement program funding problems in the future. The very real risk that China, not the US, will be the big winner of this century, could cause our workers to suffer enormously, making meaningful contributions to Social Security and Medicare nearly impossible.

Suddenly, the assumed 1.5 percent real economic growth rate questioned by the conservatives pushing their privatization scheme seems overly optimistic. Real GDP growth could be much slower as the baby boomers retire, and could even turn negative during economic shocks like the current housing crash.

The solution will not be found if Obama relies solely on the AARP to make decisions for us regarding our retirement programs. The AARP only speaks for current and near retirees, and is little interested in the tax burden on younger and poorer Americans. Obama would be smart to recognize the damage that all special interests like the AARP do to our ability to govern fairly and not just focus on corporate-backed lobbying, although there is no question that corporate lobbying is much more damaging to good governance than people-backed organizations.

But if President Obama is willing to take serious steps, such as assign payroll taxes to salary earnings over $100,000, there are real solutions to be found. The main problems we face in America today aren't economic or environmental, as great as those problems are. The biggest problem is our having to deal with the character of our politicians in Washington and, mirroring that, the character of Americans everywhere, who must be willing and able to make the hard choices to find the solutions that will overcome the massive challenges before us.

Chapter Nine

COOPERATION IS THE KEY

Our individualism has always been bound by a set of communal values, the glue upon which every healthy society depends. We value the imperatives of family and the cross-generational obligations that family implies. We value community, the neighborliness that expresses itself to raising the barn or coaching the soccer team. We value patriotism and the obligations of citizenship, a sense of duty and sacrifice on behalf of our nation. We value a faith in something bigger than ourselves, whether that something expresses itself in formal religion or ethical precepts. And we value the constellation of behaviors that express our mutual regard for one another: honesty, fairness, humility kindness, courtesy, and compassion.[1]

A major theme running through much of Obama's writings, books and speeches is an emphasis on cooperation.[2] This focus is evident in his campaign style: he is careful not to openly offend those he disagrees with, because he knows he may have to work side-by-side with them in the future to find solutions to our most pressing problems. He tries to keep his debates and disagreements from becoming personal, instead focusing on issues. Once name-calling starts and people break off into sides anticipating a fight, it is very difficult to get them to cooperate later on. If we label people as liberal or conservative, unpatriotic or reactionary, it makes it all that more difficult to break through these labels and work together down the road.

Obama did not invent this persona just for the campaign. People who knew him in law school say that he was always good at listening to all sides and bringing people of disparate views together. In his community organizing work in Chicago, cooperation was the key to getting anything done in his inner city poor neighborhood. Poor people don't have a lot of money and power. That's why they're called poor. So to garner any power needed to improve the neighborhood and increase economic opportunity for the people living there, neighbors have to learn to cooperate. That is the basis of community organizing: teaching people who have little influence on their own that together, through cooperation, they can make great progress.

A community organizer is an expert, of sorts, in understanding how to get people to cooperate. Obama is proud of his community organizing background, as can be seen in the following magazine article excerpt:

> . . . Obama connects his past as a Chicago organizer to his presidential bid with surprising ease. . . . When I began to suggest links between his organizing work then and his current campaign, he interrupted: "I think there is. I don't think you need to strain for it."
>
> . . . Publicly, as well, Obama has made his organizing days central to his political identity. When he announced his candidacy for president last month, he said the "best education" he ever had was not his undergraduate years at Occidental and Columbia or even his time at Harvard Law School, but rather the four years he spent in the mid-'80s learning the science of community organizing in Chicago. . . .
>
> Obama's self-conception as an organizer isn't just a campaign gimmick. Organizing remained central to Obama long after his stint on the South Side. . . . After he was elected to the US Senate, his wife, Michelle, told a reporter, "Barack is not a politician first and foremost. He's a community activist exploring the viability of politics to

make change." Recalling her remark in 2005, Obama wrote, "I take that observation as a compliment."[3]

Effective organizing is about getting people to cooperate and to understand how their self-interest will be satisfied by a group solution, but Obama also believes it is about getting people to realize that they share common principles and goals and that advancing the group is also an admirable goal.[4] Selflessness is always a more difficult sell than selfishness, but both can be satisfied through effective cooperation. Of course, one of the keys to convincing people to cooperate together is effective leadership. The importance of an inspirational leader that can convince us that we are all in this together, and that if we act we can conquer the biggest threats to our prosperity, cannot be understated. All of Obama's speaking talents, personality characteristics and motivational and inspirational skills will be needed to bring us all together to work for a common cause.

Listed below is my attempt to generate a list of the 25 Greatest Threats to Our Prosperity, ranked by a hypothetical worst case cost, which is nothing more than a back of the envelope guesstimate of what the potential total cost might be over time. While certain to be highly controversial, it is meant as only an order of magnitude expression of potential costs over time, knowing that others might disagree with the ranking and the cost estimates. Part of the reason for creating such a table is to encourage such disagreement and debate that is healthy and productive. If we can't even decide which are the biggest problems facing us, how can we be expected to prioritize them, or attack them, and find solutions? Please realize these hypothetical costs are presented in trillions of dollars, so all threats on these pages are meaningful and quite large. The table also makes the point nicely that all of these issues are, in fact, economic as they all have real dollar costs associated with them. I have included a column that highlights those areas in which Obama has issued a major policy statement, to demonstrate that these are not just my ideas, but Obama's as well.

25 GREATEST THREATS TO OUR PROSPERITY

Rank	Name of Threat	Potential Cost (trillions US$)	Obama Has Made a Major Policy Statement
1	World Poverty	$100	Yes
2	Global Warming	$60	Yes
3	Globalization's Nasty Side Effects	$60	Yes
4	Political Corruption	$50	Yes
5	Human Rights Violations	$50	Yes
6	Uncontrolled Growth and Population	$50	No
7	Decline of Education	$50	Yes
8	International Trade With China	$50	Yes
9	Aging of Population	$40	Yes
10	Weak Energy Policy	$40	Yes
11	Demise of Workers' Rights	$40	Yes
12	Pollution and Environmental Degradation	$20	Yes
13	Animal Rights	$20	Yes/No[5]
14	World Health Problems	$20	Yes
15	Prejudice, Racism and the Minority	$20	Yes
16	Imperialism	$20	Yes
17	Tax Policy and Deficits	$15	Yes
18	Housing and Financial Crisis	$10	Yes
19	Commercialization of Media	$10	Yes[6]
20	War	$10	Yes
21	Religious Fundamentalism	$10	Yes
22	Alcohol, Drugs, Crime and Prison	$10	Yes
23	Tobacco Use	$10	No[7]
24	Weapons of Mass Destruction	$10	Yes
25	Terrorism	$5	Yes

One might be surprised to see both weapons of mass destruction (WMD) and terrorism ranked as low as twenty-fourth and twenty-fifth as potential threats in this table given their constant exposure in the media as very serious threats to the peace and stability of the world. In the table, this exposure to WMD and terrorism is quantified at $10 trillion and $5 trillion, respectively, which in absolute dollars is highly significant. The fact that the other threats listed in the table have even larger costs assigned to them should not diminish the public's perceived risk of WMD and terrorism, but should provide a valuable benchmark by which the sheer magnitude of the danger inherent in the other listed threats can be judged.

Werner Hans Erhard, the founder of est training, formally launched in 1977 an attempt to end world hunger by the year 2000 called The Hunger Project, Erhard was drawn to the fact that there was enough food grown on the planet each year to feed everyone, but that many still starved.[8] His solution was that the world's hunger problem could simply be willed away if enough people took responsibility for realizing the problem was conquerable and dedicated themselves to attacking it.

I don't want to be placed in the company of people like Erhard, who started life as Jack Rosenberg, a used car and encyclopedia salesman, and has been widely reported to be a fraud and a huckster, but it is just possible he was onto something. No, hunger cannot be willed away. It exists not because of inadequate foodstuffs, but because the world's poor have inadequate incomes to buy sufficient food to feed their families. International aid programs that depend on grants and food distribution ease suffering in the short term, but do little to address the fundamental problem that many of the world's poor are working hard, but just not producing and earning sufficiently to provide for their families.

But, as Erhard implies, the key to the solution to many of the complex problems we face today may lie within ourselves, and blame should not so easily be shifted to our corrupt governments or our greedy capitalist enterprises. We cannot just will away these problems, but a healthy shift in the focus of our energy, efforts and motivations toward cooperation might be the critical element necessary to generate effective solutions. If you trace these greatest threats back to their root causes, you see that, yes, corporate greed and politicians' ruthlessness contribute, but ultimately it is the people who have decided which course they want their governments to pursue, and what objectives they wish society to focus on.

It turns out that the same thing is needed to solve each of these important problems: greater global cooperation. Individual effort won't do it. The problems are too large and too complex. A single citizen who tries on his own to work toward a solution will either see very little benefit, or in fact, may face a competitive disadvantage relative to those who ignore the problems. In the parlance of economics, all of these are collective action problems, because individuals acting in their own self-interest will arrive at an equilibrium solution that is not as good for all than if the participants had cooperated and acted together.

These problems have not been solved because 1) the free market's individual participants were not motivated monetarily to find a cooperative solution, 2) the US government was too busy taking industry's money to focus on issues of importance to its people, 3) all governments are poorly organized to begin with as they have no quantitative measurement system to reward and punish, and, 4) many of these problems involve international cooperation beyond the scope of any one people's government.

Of course, it is too much to ask of Obama to solve all of these world problems. But one can find some comfort in knowing that once we establish a system for global cooperation to solve one of them, we can utilize the same approach for most of the others. While the United Nations has been the most effective international policy-making organization we have, many of the world's tyrannies and dictatorships are also represented there, making democratic and economic reform difficult.

Obama, at a speech in New York in September 2007, addressed why we all are in it together, and why cooperation is so important when it comes to achieving economic prosperity for the country:

> But I also know that in this country, our grand experiment has only worked because we have guided the market's invisible hand with a higher principle.
>
> It's the idea that we are all in this together. From CEOs '

to shareholders, from financiers to factory workers, we all have a stake in each other's success because the more Americans prosper, the more America prospers.

We have not come this far because we practice survival of the fittest. America is America because we believe in creating a framework in which all can succeed. Our free market was never meant to be a free license to take whatever you can get, however you can get it. And so from time to time, we have put in place certain rules of the road to make competition fair, and open, and honest. We have done this not to stifle prosperity or liberty, but to foster those things and ensure that they are shared and spread as widely as possible.

In recent years, we have seen a dangerous erosion of the rules and principles that have allowed our market to work and our economy to thrive. Instead of thinking about what's good for America or what's good for business, a mentality has crept into certain corners of Washington and the business world that says, "what's good for me is good enough."

In our government, we see campaign contributions and lobbyists used to cut corners and win favors that stack the deck against businesses and consumers who play by the rules.

In the business world, it's a mentality that sees conflicts of interest as opportunities for profit. The quick kill is prized without regard to long-term consequences for the financial system and the economy. And while this may benefit the few who push the envelope as far as it will go, it's doesn't benefit America and it doesn't benefit the market. Just because it makes money doesn't mean it's good for business.[9]

Addressing the trust that was broken in the subprime mortgage debacle, Obama continued:

In this modern, interconnected economy, there is no dividing line between Main Street and Wall Street. The decisions that are made in New York's high-rises and hedge funds matter and have consequences for millions of Americans across the country. And whether those Americans keep their homes or their jobs; whether they can spend with confidence and avoid falling into debt—that matters and has consequences for the entire market.

We all have a stake in each other's success. We all have a stake in ensuring that the market is efficient and transparent; that it inspires trust and confidence; that it rewards those who are truly successful instead of those who are just successful at gaming the system. Because if the last few months have taught us anything, it's that we can all suffer from the excesses of a few. Turning a blind eye to the cronyism in our midst can put us all in jeopardy. And we cannot accept that in the United States of America. . . .

But today I am asking you to join me in saying that in this country, we will not tolerate a market that is fixed. We will not tolerate a market that is rigged by lobbyists who don't represent the interests of real Americans or most businesses. And we will not tolerate "what's good for me is good enough" any longer—because the only thing that's good enough is what's best for America.

I am also asking you to join me in doing something else today. I am asking you to remind yourselves that in this country, we rise or fall as one people.

Even if citizens overcome their selfish nature and possess a real desire to discover cooperative solutions to problems facing them, there are still real impediments that make a cooperative solution difficult to implement, enforce and maintain. Obama is very familiar with these impediments, given his work in community organizing. The first of them is the size of the community. The larger the community, the more difficult to enact cooperative efforts, all other factors being constant.

Of course, there are many different sized groupings that benefit from cooperation. There are immediate and extended families, neighborhoods, work environments, cities, states, nations and the planet. We have seen that each of the twenty-five greatest threats we face today has an international component to it, and so each is dealing with the largest community of all, the global community. If increasing size of community is indeed an impediment to cooperation, than one would expect problems affecting numerous countries of the world to be some of the most difficult to cooperatively organize to solve. Reputations are an asset we carry through life, and therefore the smaller the community, the higher likelihood that good and bad actions will reflect back on the individual's reputation. And so, the larger the community, the greater the anonymity, the lower the probability that transgressors will have to suffer any consequences from their selfish, uncooperative acts.

As problems reach national and international scope in size, it is very difficult for cooperation to occur without democracy. A country's citizens can't just call a national town hall meeting to discuss their concerns. They must have in place some method of having the collective voice of the people reach their elected representatives and be heard. This is why a free press, civil liberties, and elections are so important, not only for democracy, but for any cooperative effort among citizens. Cooperation is a necessary ingredient for successful democracy, but for large scale countries and regions, democratic institutions are also essential to encouraging cooperative solutions to problems. No other societal organizing principle other than democracy can assure that the people are deciding issues most important to them, and without democratic institutions there can be no broad cooperation among citizens spread over vast distances. This is why it is disturbing that most Americans get their news from media owned and controlled by big American corporations. They would be the last to suggest limiting lobbying power of the media or other corporations, or to suggest an increase in the minimum wage.

Some have begun to suggest that the key to regaining control of global problems may lie in building stronger democratic institutions between nations. The UN could be more democratic by prohibiting membership to autocratic countries. The World Bank, the International Monetary Fund (IMF) and the World Trade Organization (WTO) could all afford to be more transparent in their decision-making, more democratic in the election of their officers, and more responsive to the peoples, rather than the corporations of the world. Some have suggested increased powers for the World Court to prevent genocide and war crimes.

The problem, of course, is that when institutions are created that exceed the boundaries of democratic countries, it is not at all clear how democracy itself will survive. Does a World Court have jurisdiction in the United States? Can it rule that our democratically determined laws of our country are unlawful by some higher international standard? Can it rule a country's constitution to be unlawful and force it to be amended? From what election do international institutions' officials gain their democratic legitimacy? Who polices a UN? Who elected its representatives, and which electorates do they report to?

And so, it may be that a one-world government and trade without borders is not ideal. Just as economists suggested once that there were optimal currency areas, there might also be optimal democracy areas. All of Europe under one union may make it more competitive, economically speaking, but it will run the risk of losing much of the democratic foundation that gives European countries their legitimacy. India's billion plus people may be too much for any one democracy to handle. The United States might become more democratic by returning much of its federal power to the states if it cannot correct the gross negligence and corruption in its federal government in Washington.

Obama knows that there may be no greater force for evil on our planet than corruption. Business cannot effectively operate in an environment of corruption, governments become impotent, citizens become apathetic, and many countries, including some of the world's richest, stagnate at less than optimal levels of productivity and happiness.

Solving complex problems in a world infested with corrupt activity is nearly impossible. The spirit of cooperation required for the effort is stymied in a world in which individuals, especially those holding powerful positions in government and industry, cheat and lie to satisfy their narrow self-interests.

While it is rational for individuals to cease cooperation with corrupt governments and organizations, the damage to society is much more broadly felt. Corruption is both an impediment to cooperation in a society, and a symptom that something in society has gone terribly wrong. It appears on our list of the twenty-five greatest threats to our prosperity, but it also acts as a devious threat to the solution— namely, greater societal cooperation. To effectively solve these major world problems we need cooperation, and yet one of the very problems we are trying to solve, corruption, has a cancerous effect on cooperation itself. If people believe society is corrupt, they will choose not to cooperate, and yet without cooperation there can be no chance of attacking corruption. This is why corruption might be the most difficult of all of these threats to our society; it acts to prevent the cooperative effort that is required in order to conquer it.

Corruption, unfortunately, is not limited to the developing world. What other word applies to an American Congress that regularly accepts campaign donations in exchange for favorable legislation to industry, tax cuts to rich contributors, and trade agreements that abuse the poorest countries on our planet? While corruption may be more widespread in the developing world, corruption in America and other advanced countries is more sophisticated and better hidden.

The greater the level of trust within a community-oriented group, and the more trustworthy the individual participants, the more likely that cooperation will occur amongst them. Because effective cooperation involves the expectation that others will cooperate also, the more tight-knit the group, the more likely its members will assume others will also cooperate. In effect, if the group is strong, then participants will assume that other group members will think like they do and come to the rational decision that it is better to cooperate than not. Obama, with his black, white, Asian, and mixed-race relatives, understands this perfectly. His solution is to get Americans to look past their differences, especially in ethnic background, and come together to solve these important problems through cooperative effort.

Finally, people are more willing to cooperate if they think they can win. Obama learned this in community organizing, where the rule is take small steps at first, allowing the group to win a few, and then move to more complex issues once the group's confidence is high. Obama's campaign slogan echoed the winning sentiment, "Yes We Can!" While we can hope that mankind will become more compassionate and show greater concern for the welfare of others over time, realistically, it must be said that the primary reason that people cooperate is to improve their own lot. An effective organizer of cooperative effort understands that the way to encourage participation by the group is to show them that by joining together, they are maximizing their own well-being. A true win-win situation. Obama is not going to begin by being combative, fighting toe to toe with big business to stop their lobbying in Washington. He is going to explain to them that it is the wrong thing to do and that in the long run it weakens America by misallocating resources and damaging the motivation and work ethic of the American people.

If we make this cooperative effort and solve some of these devastating problems, we will have created a greater and more just society, and we will indeed benefit tremendously. Besides the enormous sense of pride and accomplishment that will result from solving these matters, we will be eliminating many of the threats that face our country, our children, and the planet.

Chapter Ten

ETHICS AND ECONOMICS: MY BROTHER'S KEEPER

. . . For alongside our famous individualism, there's another ingredient in the American saga. A belief that we are connected as one people. If there's a child on the south side of Chicago who can't read, that matters to me, even if it's not my child. If there's a senior citizen somewhere who can't pay for her prescription and has to choose between medicine and the rent, that makes my life poorer, even if it's not my grandmother. If there's an Arab American family being rounded up without benefit of an attorney or due process, that threatens my civil liberties. It's that fundamental belief—I am my brother's keeper, I am my sister's keeper—that makes this country work. It's what allows us to pursue our individual dreams, yet still come together as a single American family. E pluribus Unum. Out of many, one.[1]

If you ask a typical resident of Buenos Aires what is wrong with Argentina, and why it languishes in its economic development at a level of productivity and income approximately equal to one quarter of the advanced world, you will hear a litany of responses. Some blame the corruption of the justice system, including its judges and its police force; others cite a one-party political system, or a passive wealthy elite that controls the vast majority of the natural resource, real estate, and financial wealth in the country. Even the dirt poor picaderos living on the street get blamed by some, as they have no jobs and are drawing a small $50.00 per month benefit from the government.

In the US, posing a similar question as to why Americans are unhappy with such vast wealth and opportunity generates an equally long list of possible culprits. The American government is corrupted by special interests, especially large corporations. The business community is chasing short-term profits instead of creating long-term values, and globalization is stealing our jobs. The news media is more interested in making profits than reporting the news. Communities are collapsing, no one knows their neighbors anymore, and the public school system is an abject failure.

So these two disparate countries, Argentina and the United States, find themselves similar in one very important aspect. When asked the cause of their problems their citizens blame almost everyone but themselves. Never in the history of the world has someone said in response to the question of what is wrong with his country that it was his own fault—or, more literally, the fault of the general population, including myself. The people number in the tens and hundreds of millions and don't exercise their power. The only thing worse than the widespread corruption of public officials in Argentina is that nobody speaks out against it. It has become part of the system. The only thing worse than the atrocities committed at Abu Ghraib prison in Iraq by American military personnel is the lack of revulsion and demonstrations in the street by Americans when they heard the news.

The greatest threats facing our nation today require action by the American people, and before there can be real action there must be a sense of moral outrage. And this does not mean only among the disenfranchised, but also from middle-class and affluent American citizens who are sick and tired of living in an immoral, unjust and uncaring world. There is no problem in the world today, however large and threatening, that can withstand the outrage of the people once they've decided that they have had enough and are ready to take action. The important question is, why should we be concerned about the welfare of others? Why would someone in his right mind ever elevate the well-being of others, especially strangers, over his own self-interest? Obama gave a speech on July 18, 2007 in Washington, DC on urban economic opportunity in which he tried to address some of these difficult questions:

> We can't allow this kind of suffering and hopelessness to exist in our country. We can't afford to lose a generation of tomorrow's doctors and scientists and teachers to poverty. We can make excuses for it or we can fight about it or we can ignore poverty altogether, but as long as it's here it will always be a betrayal of the ideals we hold as Americans. It's not who we are. In this country—of all countries—no child's destiny should be determined before he takes his first step. No little girl's future should be confined to the neighborhood she was born into . . .[2]

One out of every eight Americans lives in poverty, defined as a family of four trying to live on approximately $19,000 per year. This rate has doubled since 1980. Obama described the role of government in solving the poverty problem in America, saying, "When you're in these neighborhoods, you can see what a difference it makes to have a government that cares. You can see what a free lunch program does for a hungry child. You can see what a little extra money from an earned income tax credit does for a family that's struggling. You can see what prenatal care does for the health of a mother and a newborn. So don't tell me there's no role for government in lifting up our cities."

But he also challenged Americans to act responsibly and morally. He was not just asking the wealthy to become more involved; in his talk he also asked the poor to take more responsibility and act more ethically towards each other. "But you can also see what a difference it makes when people start caring for themselves. It makes a difference when a father realizes that responsibility does not end at conception; when he understands that what makes you a man is not the ability to have a child, but the courage to raise one. It makes a difference when a parent turns off the TV once in awhile, puts away the video games, and starts reading to their child, and getting involved in his education. . . ."[3]

Organized religions have very neat reasons why we should act morally and show concern for our fellow man—such as, you will burn in hell if you don't. While religion often gets much of the moral message right—no killing, no lying, no cheating—much of the moral importance in our lives has been lost as we look less and less to our churches for advice and guidance in our lives. In today's highly scientific, highly individualistic, highly skeptical culture, many end up dismissing religion in their lives as they lose confidence in a system so highly dependent on faith rather than logical proof. Faith sounds wonderful to the faithful, but to the uninitiated it is an excuse to avoid rational reasoning in defending one's actions. How many times have you heard that the reason we should do things a certain way is because that is how it was done in the Good Book, or that is what Jesus would have done, or that to do otherwise would violate religious law?

And so, as many turn away from religion, they never develop a deeper understanding of why they should continue to act morally and ethically. Is there a reason to lead a good moral life that is not based solely on religious teachings? Certainly we know that it is human nature that we just might feel good by helping others, but this feel good approach is itself too self serving. Is there a reason to show concern for others, even if we don't feel good inside when we do? What if we weren't hard-wired by genetics to do at least some minimal cooperating? Is there a good rational reason to help others and try to solve our global problems regardless of what our genes want us to do?

We may realize that it is just smart to do so and that it is in our own self-interest. By attacking world poverty, we will eliminate some of the conditions that incite terrorism. By addressing world health issues, we will make ourselves safe from unknown globally contagious viruses and epidemics. And by addressing society's concerns now rather than leaving them for our children's generation, we may prevent future social unrest and revolt that could rob us of our sacred status and precious material possessions.

But what if we weren't going to benefit personally from addressing these world problems? What if the total benefit accrued solely to the harmed, the sick, the elderly, the poor, the disenfranchised, and our children, and there was no secondary benefit that might accrue back to us? If we can show that there is a reason and motivation for moral action and concern for others, even in the absence of self-interest, than this will be a compelling argument to find solutions to the threats facing us today, and to do so immediately.

The fundamental reason why each of us is driven and motivated to act morally is that we are not alone. We inhabit this planet with six billion other people and countless other species of animals, all of whom wish to be treated well. We ourselves wish to be treated well, but isn't it internally illogical to demand that we be treated well by others and yet not return the favor and treat them well also? Almost all of ethical action can be summarized by the simple thought experiment of putting yourself in the other person's shoes. If we can do this simple mental exercise, we can begin to see how we would like to be treated if we were in the other's situation. Only then can we develop the empathy necessary to see that compassion and care for the disadvantaged and helpless isn't just compassionate, it is logical. Even if we are certain that we ourselves will never be in a position in which we would be in need, by putting ourselves in the other person's shoes we can begin to understand that ending human suffering is everybody's job. As Obama says, "In the end, then, what is called for is nothing more, and nothing less, than what all the world's great religions demand—that we do unto others as we would have them do unto us. Let us be our brother's keeper. . . . Let us be our sister's keeper. Let us find that common stake we all have in one another, and let our politics reflect that spirit as well."[4]

If we were poor, we wouldn't want equality of pay or charity from the rich, but we might want a helping hand until things got better, we might want a job that paid a living wage, and we might want an economic system that was fair and just so that our children had as much opportunity as anyone of succeeding in the future. If we were poor and sick, we wouldn't want expensive medical procedures and pharmaceuticals and access to medical specialists given to us for free, but we might want a minimum level of medical care for our children and families, and access to cheaper generic forms of medicines. If we were old, we wouldn't want to get rich off a bankrupt retirement system that was harming our grandchildren, but we might want to know that if things went bad, someone would be there to look out for us.

And so the lesson is not that we might be poor in the future so we better make sure the poor are taken care of, although there is some obvious logic in this way of thinking. No, the lesson is that even if we are certain we will never be poor, we still have an obligation to care for the poor today. The very logical reason is that we are an understanding species capable of critical thought. If we utilize our brains by putting ourselves in the other person's shoes and asking how their suffering feels, we will very quickly realize that empathy is not an illogical emotion that runs counter to our self-interest. Rather, empathy is fundamental and logical, and leads to moral action and concern for others specifically because we understand and comprehend human suffering, its consequences, the pain it causes, its inherent unfairness and unjustness, and are repelled by it regardless of who has to be its victim. Tom Joad in John Steinbeck's magnificent novel, *The Grapes of Wrath*, had it right after all.[5]

> . . . Ma. I've been thinkin' a hell of a lot, thinkin about our people livin' like pigs, an' the good rich lan' layin' fallow, or maybe one fella with a million acres, while a hundred thou-

san' good farmers is starvin.' An' I been wonderin' if all our
folks got together an' yelled, like them fellas yelled. . . .

Well, maybe like Casy says, a fella ain't got a soul of his
own, but on'y a piece of a big one—an' then—then it don'
matter. And I'll be all aroun' in the dark. I'll be ever'where—
wherever you look. Wherever they's a fight so hungry
people can eat, I'll be there. Wherever they's a cop beating
up a guy, I'll be there. If Casy knowed, why, I'll be in the way
guys yell when they're mad an'—I'll be in the way kids laugh
when they're hungry an' they know supper's ready. An' when
our folks eat the stuff they raise an' live in the houses they
build—why, I'll be there. See? God, I'm talkin' like Casy.

What other true calling can there be in life when your fellow
man is hurting, but to use your energy and effort to alleviate his
suffering? No wonder self-interested action that ignores societies'
greatest problems pales in comparison and results in feelings of
unfulfilled emptiness. The curse, of course, is that once you recognize this simple truth about the importance of empathy, you will
no longer be happy at the beauty parlor getting your hair done,
wasting hours in front of the TV, shopping at the mall, or loung-
ing about your big house in the suburbs. The world is calling you.
Are you going to answer the call?

If we can agree that there are very good rational empathetic reasons and motivations as to why we should act morally, even in the
absence of religion and any indirect benefits to ourselves, then let
us turn to how we can stimulate greater moral action in general.
Greater moral outrage, action, and cooperation are the keys to
solving the great problems facing our society today. Problems
affecting our innocent children and problems impacting mainly the
poor and sick most likely will not be addressed if we rely solely on
pursuing our narrowly defined self-interest. The motivation for
such unselfish action must be moral in nature.

According to people who know him, Obama is great at getting

people motivated and angry enough to take action. Below is a short excerpt from a *New Republic* article describing his introduction to community organizing in Chicago.

> Not long after Obama arrived [in Chicago], he sat down for a cup of coffee in Hyde Park with a fellow organizer named Mike Kruglik. Obama's work focused on helping poor blacks on Chicago's South Side fight the city for things like job banks and asbestos removal. His teachers were schooled in a style of organizing devised by Saul Alinsky, the radical University of Chicago trained social scientist. At the heart of the Alinsky method is the concept of "agitation"—making someone angry enough about the rotten state of his life that he agrees to take action to change it; or, as Alinsky himself described the job, to "rub raw the sores of discontent."
>
> On this particular evening, Kruglik was debriefing Obama about his work when a panhandler approached. Instead of ignoring the man, Obama confronted him. "Now, young man, is that really what you want to be about?" Obama demanded. "I mean, come on, don't you want to be better than that? Let's get yourself together."
>
> Kruglik remembers this episode as an example of why, in ten years of training organizers, Obama was the best student he ever had. He was a natural, the undisputed master of agitation, who could engage a room full of recruiting targets in a rapid-fire Socratic dialogue, nudging them to admit that they were not living up to their own standards. As with the panhandler, he could be aggressive and confrontational. With probing, sometimes personal questions, he would pinpoint the source of pain in their lives, tearing down their egos just enough before dangling a carrot of hope that they could make things better.[6]

Of course any good moral education starts at home. In his book, *The Audacity of Hope*, Obama has an entire chapter on family in which he discusses the importance of being there for your children.[7] He says it is not only his priority to raise his daughters properly, but his wife Michelle would only allow the presidential bid if it did not interfere with the raising of their children.[8] We should be concerned that many of our bedtime stories, fables and myths we tell our children, many with strong moral lessons attached, are being replaced by rap videos, violent television and cinema, and vacuous video games of little to no moral value. It is not that these art forms should be outlawed, it is just that parents should be able to make informed decisions to decide at what age children should be exposed to them. It is a shame that children are reading less, because fictional novels are a wonderful way to improve one's empathy skills and learn to examine problems from another's perspective, even if it just a fictional character facing a moral crisis.

Each of the problems we face as a society has a tipping point phenomena associated with it. Explained by Malcolm Gladwell in his book of the same name,[9] the tipping point refers to collective problems that essentially remain inertially immovable until a certain percentage of the population adopts the solution, at which point there is a steamroller effect and all resistance evaporates. The status quo is a powerful force to overcome, and many of us are more followers than leaders, so real popular support for your initiatives won't come until you achieve this critical mass. The good news is that a relatively few people can achieve rather dramatic change in society by operating around these fulcrums or tipping points and causing a dramatic change in the overall direction of society. Gandhi in India's fight for freedom, Rosa Parks in the US Civil Rights movement, and of course, Martin Luther King with his insistence on non-violent change, all come to mind as people who manipulated society just beyond the tipping point and thus successfully changed its direction forever.

As usual, Obama says it better than I ever could.

This was one of the tasks we set forth at the beginning of this campaign—to continue the long march of those who came before us, a march for a more just, more equal, more free, more caring, and more prosperous America. I chose to run for the presidency at this moment in history because I believe deeply that we cannot solve the challenges of our time unless we solve them together—unless we perfect our union by understanding that we may have different stories, but we hold common hopes; that we may not look the same and we may not have come from the same place, but we all want to move in the same direction—towards a better future for our children and our grandchildren.

This belief comes from my unyielding faith in the decency and generosity of the American people. But it also comes from my own American story . . .

It's a story that hasn't made me the most conventional candidate. But it is a story that has seared into my genetic makeup the idea that this nation is more than the sum of its parts—that out of many, we are truly one."[10]

We will not have a prosperous economy, a healthy people, or a great nation until we understand that we are all in this together. It is more of a boating race than a foot race in that there won't be one runner who sprints the fastest and beats the rest; rather, we can only win if everyone in the boat rows hard together, knowing that we will cross the finish line together or sink trying.

Obama spoke to college students in Mount Vernon, Iowa on the nation's call to service in 2007. He wanted to instill the idea in these young students that it was not their country's responsibility to solve their problems—it was their responsibility. Here is the conclusion of his remarks to the students that day.

. . . You go to the first school in the United States west of the Mississippi to grant women the same rights and privileges as men. You go to a school that resolved in 1870 that race would not be a factor in admission. These may be small changes on the vast canvas of history, but the America we live in is the sum total of that kind of courage, that spirit of progress. If it weren't for that kind of change, it wouldn't be possible for someone like me to stand here today to talk to you about the future of this country. You and I are at a place where somebody, at some point, decided that loving their community and their country meant doing something to change it.

Renewing that spirit starts with service. Make no mistake: our destiny as Americans is tied up with one another. If we are less respected in the world, then you will be less safe. If we keep paying dictators to fill up our gas tanks, then those oceans are going to rise. If we can't give our kids a world-class education, then our economy is going to fall behind. . . .

That's what history calls us to do. Because loving your country shouldn't just mean watching fireworks on the fourth of July; loving your country must mean accepting your responsibility to do your part to change it. And if you do stand up, I promise you that your life will be richer, and our country will be stronger.

We need your service, right now, in this moment—our moment—in history. I'm not going to tell you what your role should be; that's for you to discover. But I am going to ask you to play your part; ask you to stand up; ask you to put your foot firmly into the current of history. I am asking you to change history's course.[II]

EPILOGUE

. . . Most of the time I stop at the Washington Monument, but sometimes I push on, across the street to the National World War II Memorial, then along the reflecting pool to the Vietnam Veterans Memorial, then up the stairs of the Lincoln Memorial . . .

And in that place, I think about America and those who built it. This nation's founders, who somehow rose above petty ambitions and narrow calculations to imagine a nation unfurling across a continent. And those like Lincoln and King, who ultimately laid down their lives in the service of perfecting an imperfect union. And all the faceless, nameless men and women, slaves and soldiers and tailors and butchers, constructing lives for themselves and their children and their grandchildren, brick by brick, rail by rail, calloused hand by calloused hand, to fill in the landscape of our collective dreams.

It is that process I wish to be a part of. My heart is filled with love for this country.[1]

There remains only one question. Can he pull it off? Or, as Obama would prefer, can we pull it off? In trying to clean up Washington and limit the power of special interests, he will be going up against one hundred senators and 435 congressmen, each of whom is dependent on special interests to fund their campaigns. It is not as simple as getting these congressional leaders to agree to a cease-fire amongst themselves on campaign spending. They are not competing for reelection with each other. Rather, they are incumbents competing against non-incumbents. In other words, campaign donations from special interests don't necessarily help Democrats or Republicans more, but they certainly help incumbents more. If Obama is going to receive support from the Congress, he has to figure out some way of addressing this issue, because the incumbents in Washington will not favor reform that decreases their chance at reelection.

If Obama goes after the special interests, he will be taking on almost all of corporate America, including Wall Street, the health-care industry, the real estate lobby, and so on, as well as the most powerful political organizations of citizens in the country including our largest labor unions, our teacher unions, the AARP, and the environmental lobby. If one were a betting man, and you had not heard Obama speak, common sense would dictate that you would have to bet against him, given the power of his opponents and the intransigence of the status quo. But now that we have heard Obama speak, and we understand his vision and see its appeal with the American public, you cannot be so sure that he might not be the one capable of accomplishing this major reform to our government, and the one who returns decency, honesty, and justice to Washington. He just might deliver.

The best Obama speech during the presidential campaign was not given by Barack, but by his wife Michelle. It was given without notes or teleprompter on February 3, 2008 at UCLA in Los Angeles, the Sunday morning before super Tuesday, when she was joined onstage by Oprah Winfrey, Caroline Kennedy, and Maria Shriver. It was a convincing and winning pitch that her husband was the man for the job, and that he was really capable of rallying the people behind him and building a coalition strong enough to take our country back from the special interests:

> In 2008, we are still a nation that is too divided. We live in
> isolation, and because of that isolation, we fear one another.
> We don't know our neighbors, we don't talk, we believe our
> pain is our own. We don't realize that the struggles and

challenges of all of us are the same. We are too isolated. And we are still a nation that is still too cynical. We look at it as "them" and "they" as opposed to "us" . . .

We have lost the understanding that in a democracy, we have a mutual obligation to one another—that we cannot measure the greatness of our society by the strongest and richest of us, but we have to measure our greatness by the least of these. That we have to compromise and sacrifice for one another in order to get things done. That is why I am here, because Barack Obama is the only person in this who understands that. That before we can work on the problems, we have to fix our souls. Our souls are broken in this nation.

Barack Obama will require you to work. He is going to demand that you shed your cynicism. That you put down your divisions. That you come out of your isolation, that you move out of your comfort zones. That you push yourselves to be better. And that you engage. Barack will never allow you to go back to your lives as usual, uninvolved, uninformed.[2]

Michelle said that Barack had wisdom, and that wisdom was not something you acquired through years on a job; you either had it or you didn't. She was not shy at all about her conviction that her husband was the only person that could do this job. And she said, we will only get one shot at this, hinting that she was not going to allow her husband time away from their children to run again if for some reason it didn't work out this time. She knew what many people surmised—that her husband was the real thing, and that she had complete confidence in his ability to pull this off.

When Bill Richardson endorsed Barack Obama for president, he said, "Your candidacy is a once-in-a-lifetime opportunity for our country, and you are a once-in-a-lifetime leader."[3] There was John Kennedy and his brother Bobby, there was Martin Luther King, Jr.

and then there was a void. What they shared in common, and Obama seems to also share, is a deep abiding concern for all Americans and for this country based on the principles of justice, equality and opportunity that our nation was founded on. They were men of the people. They shared a common dream. Many see Obama as their heir sent here to complete work they started but left unfinished.

Obama will never pull this off without the support of the American people. But rallying their support is his strength. He will not only seek their support, he will also seek the support of the Congress, big business, the healthcare lobby, the young, the old, the news networks, employers, and employees, because he will take the time to make a very rational argument that what he proposes is the right thing to do, and show that all will benefit in the long run from a better government and a more just America. Only lobbyists on K Street will fight him on this, but in the end they will all find gainful employment utilizing their talents, whatever those may be, elsewhere.

On November 13, 2006, Barack Obama spoke at the Dr. Martin Luther King, Jr. National Memorial Groundbreaking Ceremony, and I quote:

> I have two daughters, ages five and eight. And when I see the plans for this memorial, I think about what it will be like when I first bring them here upon the memorial's completion.
>
> I imagine us walking down to this tidal basin, between one memorial dedicated to the man who helped give birth to a nation, and another dedicated to the man who preserved it . . .
>
> And at some point, I know that one of my daughters will ask, perhaps my youngest, will ask, "Daddy, why is this monument here? What did this man do?"

. . . Through words he gave voice to the voiceless. Through deeds he gave courage to the faint of heart. By dint of vision, and determination, and most of all faith in the redeeming power of love, he endured the humiliation of arrest, the loneliness of a prison cell, the constant threats to his life, until he finally inspired a nation to transform itself, and begin to live up to the meaning of its creed.

. . . a land that measured itself by how it treats the least of these, a land in which strength is defined not simply by the capacity to wage war but by the determination to forge peace—a land in which all of God's children might come together in a spirit of brotherhood . . .

As Dr. King asked to be remembered, I will tell them that this man gave his life serving others. I will tell them that this man tried to love somebody. I will tell them that because he did these things, they live today with the freedom God intended, their citizenship unquestioned, their dreams unbounded.

And I will tell them that they too can love. That they too can serve. And that each generation is beckoned anew, to fight for what is right, and strive for what is just, and to find within itself the spirit, the sense of purpose, that can remake a nation and transform a world.[4]

NOTES

INTRODUCTION

1. Charles Dickens, *A Tale of Two Cities* (New York: Penguin Classics, 2003).

2. Kevin Murphy, "What Excessive Pay Package?" *Portfolio*, June 6, 2007, http://www.portfolio.com/interactive-features/2007/06/salary_comparison.

3. George Draffan, "Facts on the Concentration of Wealth," April 2008, http://www.endgame.org/primer-wealth.html.

4. Obama for America, "Barack Obama's Plan for a Healthy America," http://www.barackobama.com/issues/pdf/HealthCareFullPlan.pdf.

5. Wikipedia, "World energy resources and consumption," April 2008, http://en.wikipedia.org/wiki/World_energy_resources_and_consumption#By_country.

6. NationMaster, "Municipal Waste Per Capita by Country," March 2008, http://www.nationmaster.com/graph/env_pol_mun_was_per_cap-pollution-municipal -waste-per-capita.

7. Wikipedia, "List of Countries by Carbon Dioxide Emissions Per Capita," 2004, http://en.wikipedia.org/wiki/List_of_countries_by_carbon_dioxide_emissions_per _capita#List_of_countries_by_emissions.

8. Peter G. Peterson, *Running On Empty: How the Democratic and Republican Parties Are Bankrupting Our Future and What Americans Can Do About It* (New York: Picador, 2005), 33.

9. Laurence J. Kotlikoff and Scott Burns, *The Coming Generational Storm: What You Need to Know about America's Economic Future* (Boston: MIT Press, 2005).

10. Roger Doyle, "By the Numbers: Can't Read, Can't Count," *Scientific American*, October 2001, http://www.sciamdigital.com/index.cfm?fa=Products.ViewIssuePreview&ISSUEID_CHAR=1353CDCA-AF4D-4B1D-85F4-5B68F2A7E17&ARTIC LEID_CHAR=E124BD2C-4169-4F9B-8C79-C06C6F11B47.

11. AssociatedPress "Young Americans Shaky on Geographic Smarts," AP, http://www .msnbc.msn.com/id/12591413/.

12. John R. Talbott, *Sell Now! The End of the Housing Bubble* (New York: St. Martin's Press, 2006).

13. Peterson, *Running On Empty*, 33.

14. Talbott, *Sell Now! The End of the Housing Bubble.*

15. Mike DeRosa, "Undercounting the Unemployed?" Green Party of Connecticut, http://www.ctgreens.org/articles/unemployed.html.

16. Barack Obama, Keynote Address, 2004 Democratic National Convention, July 2004, http://www.americanrhetoric.com/speeches/convention2004/barack-obama2004dnc.htm.

17. The Pew Research Center for the People & the Press, "Obama Weathers the Wright Storm, Clinton Faces Credibility Problem," March 27, 2008, http://people-press.org/reports/display.php3?ReportID=407.

18. Americanrhetoric.com, "Remarks of Robert F. Kennedy in Indianapolis, Indiana on April 4, 1968," April 2008, http://www.americanrhetoric.com/speeches/rfkon-mlkdeath.html.

19. John F. Kennedy Presidential Library and Museum, "Remarks of Robert F. Kennedy at the University of Capetown; Capetown, South Africa," June 6, 1966, http://www.jfklibrary.org/Historical+Resources/Archives/Reference+Desk/Speeches/RFK/Day+of+Affirmation+Address+News+Release.htm.

20. Robert F. Kennedy, "What Do We Stand For? The Liberation Of The Human Spirit," Commonwealth Club of California, 1968, http://www.commonwealth-club.org/archive/ 20thcentury/68-01kennedy-speech.html.

21. Bureau of Labor Statistics, "Consumer Price Index," US Department Of Labor, March 14, 2008, ftp://ftp.bls.gov/pub/special.requests/cpi/cpiai.txt.

22. Nancy Olsson and Ulf Johansson, "Environmental Expenditure Statistics," Eurostat, 2005, http://epp.eurostat.ec.europa.eu/pls/portal/docs/PAGE/PGP_DS_ENVACC/PGE_DS_ENVACC/TAB63667842/4.PDF.

23. Marc Kaufman and Rob Stein, "Record Share Of Economy Spent on Health Care," *Washington Post*, January 10, 2006.

24. George Orwell, *Animal Farm* (New York: Signet Books, 2004).

25. Robert F. Kennedy, "What Do We Stand For?"

26. Americanrhetoric.com, Edward M. Kennedy eulogy for Senator Robert F. Kennedy, June 8, 1968, http://www.americanrhetoric.com/speeches/ekennedytributetorfk.html.

27. Richard Holler, "Abraham, Martin, and John," Los Angeles: Laurie Records, 1968, http://www.ocap.ca/songs/abraham.html.

CHAPTER ONE—ECONOMIC JUSTICE

1. Barack Obama, Keynote Address at the 2004 Democratic National Convention, July 2004, http://www.americanrhetoric.com/speeches/convention2004/barack-obama2004dnc.htm.

2. Speech by Barack Obama, "Keeping America's Promise," Janesville General Motors Assembly Plant, February 13, 2008, http://my.barackobama.com/page/community/post/samgrahamfelsen/Cmzm.

3. Ibid.

4. Obama Campaign, "The Blueprint for Change: Barack Obama's Plan for America," Obama for America, http://www.barackobama.com/pdf/ObamaBlueprintForChange.pdf.

5. Barack Obama, *The Audacity of Hope: Thoughts on Reclaiming the American Dream* (New York: Crown Publishing Group and Three Rivers Press, 2006), 193.

6. Ibid, 8.

7. Ibid, 54-55.

8. Ibid.

9. Ibid, 7.

10. Edmund L. Andrews, "Report Finds Tax Cuts Heavily Favor The Wealthy," *New York Times*, August 13, 2004, http://query.nytimes.com/gst/fullpage.html?res=9A03 E2D6173FF930A2575BC0A9629C8B63.

11. George Draffan, "Facts on the Concentration of Wealth," March 2008, http://www.endgame.org/primer-wealth.html.

12. "Obama's Big Speech," *Portland Mercury*, quoting Barack Obama, March 21, 2008, http://blogtown.portlandmercury.com/2008/03/obamas_big_speech_2.php.

13. Obama, *The Audacity of Hope*, 63.

14. Ibid, 148.

15. Ibid, 178.

16. Daron Acemoglu, Simon Johnson, and James A. Robinson, "The Colonial Origins of Comparative Development: An Empirical Investigation," *American Economic Review*, vol. 91, December 2001, 1369-1401.

17. Daron Acemoglu, Simon Johnson, and James A. Robinson, "Reversal of Fortune: Geography and Institutions in the Making of the Modern World Income Distribution," *Quarterly Journal of Economics*, vol. 117, November 2002, 1231-1294.

18. Richard Roll and John R. Talbott, "Political Freedom, Economic Liberty, and Prosperity," *Journal of Democracy*, vol. 14, no. 3, July 2003, 75-89.

19. Talbott, *Sell Now! The End of the Housing Bubble.*

20. John R. Talbott, *The Coming Crash of the Housing Market* (New York: McGraw Hill, 2003).

21. Roll and Talbott, "Political Freedom, Economic Liberty, and Prosperity," 75–89.

22. Speech by Barack Obama, "Renewing the American Economy," Cooper Union, New York, March 27, 2008, http://www.barackobama.com/2008/03/27/remarks_of_senator_barack_obam_54.php.

23. "Carlyle Capital's Comeuppance: High Leverage Proves Onerous," *Wall Street Journal*, Breaking Views, March 7, 2008, http://online.wsj.com/article/SB12048459 0324917929.html?mod=googlenews_wsj.

24. Obama, *The Audacity of Hope*, 184.

25. Barack Obama, *Dreams From My Father: A Story of Race and Inheritance* (New York: Three Rivers Press, 1995, 2004).

26. Obama Campaign, "Restoring Trust In Government And Improving Transparency, March 2008, http://www.barackobama.com/pdf/ TakingBackOurGovernmentBack-FinalFactSheet.pdf.

27. Dennis Cauchon, "State, Local Government Workers See Pay Gains," *USA Today*, February 2008, http://www.usatoday.com/news/nation/2008-02-01-civil-servants _N.htm.

CHAPTER TWO—ECONOMIC OPPORTUNITY

1. Obama, Keynote Address, 2004 Democratic National Convention.

2. DeRosa, "Undercounting the Unemployed?"

3. United States Department of Labor, "Bureau of Labor Statistics News," April 4, 2008, http://www.bls.gov/news.release/pdf/empsit.pdf.

4. Talbott, *The Coming Crash of the Housing Market.*

5. Ibid.

6. Speech by Barack Obama. "Reclaiming the American Dream," Bettendorf, Iowa, November 7, 2007, http://www.barackObama.com/2007/11/07/remarks_of_senator _barack_obam_31.php.

7. Obama, *The Audacity of Hope*, 189–194.

8. Ibid., 190–191.

9. Obama Campaign, "Strengthening Families and Communities," March 2008, http://www.barackobama.com/issues/family/.

10. Obama Campaign, "A World Class Education," March 2008, http://www.barack-obama.com/issues/education/.

11. Ibid.

12. Ibid.

13. Speech by Barack Obama, "A More Perfect Union," Constitution Center, Philadelphia, PA, March 18, 2008, http://www.barackobama.com/2008/03/18/remarks _of_senator _barack_obam_53.php.

14. Ibid.

15. Ibid.

16. Ibid.

17. Obama Campaign, "Plan to Strengthen Civil Rights," March 2008, http://www .barackobama.com/issues/civilrights/.

18. Roll and Talbott, "Political Freedom, Economic Liberty, and Prosperity," 75–89.

19. Ibid.

20. John R. Talbott, *Where America Went Wrong: And How to Regain Her Democratic Ideals* (New York: Financial Times/Prentice Hall, 2004).

21. Obama, *The Audacity of Hope*, 137–194.

CHAPTER THREE—THE CURRENT FINANCIAL CRISIS

1. Obama, *The Audacity of Hope*, 158–159.

2. Talbott, *Sell Now! The End of the Housing Bubble*.

3. Talbott, *The Coming Crash of the Housing Market*.

4. Talbott, *Sell Now! The End of the Housing Bubble*.

5. Ibid., 91–111.

6. Ibid.

7. Obama Campaign, "Plan to Strengthen the Economy," March 2008, http://www .barack.obama.com/issues/economy/#home-ownership.

8. Ibid.

9. Floyd Norris, "IndyMac Spreads the Blame," *New York Times*, February 12, 2008, http://norris.blogs.nytimes.com/2008/02/12/indymac-spreads-the-blame/.

10. Talbott, *Sell Now! The End of the Housing Bubble*, 127–128.

11. Ibid, 32–43.

12. Obama Campaign, "Plan to Strengthen the Economy."

13. Ibid.

14. Ibid.

15. Ibid.

16. Center for Responsive Politics, "Charles E. Schumer (D-NY) Detailed Contributor Breakdown, 2000 Election Cycle," 2000, http://www.opensecrets.org/politicians/detail.asp?CID=N00001093&cycle=2000.

17. Talbott, *The Coming Crash of the Housing Market*, 129.

18. Barack Obama, "Renewing the American Economy," speech given at Cooper Union, March 27, 2008, http://www.barackobama.com/2008/03/27/remarks_of_senator_barack_obam_54.php.

19. Damian Paletta and Elizabeth Williamson, "Lobbyists, Small Banks Attack Plan For Markets," *Wall Street Journal*, April 1, 2008.

20. Jon Bruner, "Bear Stearns: What the Candidates Say," *Chicago Tribune*, March 2008, http://blogs.forbes.com/trailwatch/2008/03/bear-stearns-wh.html.

21. Obama, "Renewing the American Economy."

22. Gillian Tett, "Derivatives Market Grows by 25%," *Australian Business*, November 20, 2006, http://www.theaustralian.news.com.au/story/0,20867,20785202-36375,00.html.

CHAPTER FOUR—THE BIGGEST PROBLEM: CORPORATE LOBBYING

1. Obama for America, "Remarks of Senator Barack Obama—Iowa Jefferson-Jackson Dinner," November 10, 2007, http://www.barackobama.com/2007/11/10/remarks_of_senator_barack_obam_33.php.

2. "Lobbying Overview," opensecrets.org Lobbying Database, April 2008, http://www .opensecrets.org/lobbyists/overview.asp?showyear=a&txtindextype=s.

3. Obama Campaign, "Plan to Change Washington," April 2008, http://www .barackobama.com/issues/ethics/.

4. "Lobbying Overview," opensecrets.org Lobbying Database, April 2008, http://www .opensecrets.org/lobbyists/index.asp.

5. "Lobbying Overview," opensecrets.org Lobbying Database, April 2008, http://www .opensecrets.org/lobbyists/overview.asp?showyear=2007&txtindextype=i.

6. "Lobbying Overview," opensecrets.org Lobbying Database, April 2008, http://www .opensecrets.org/lobbyists/indusclient.asp?code=H04&year=2007.

7. John R. Talbott, *Where America Went Wrong*, 69-70.

8. Ibid.

9. Michael Powell, "Obama Is Moving to Down-to-Earth Oratory," *New York Times*, April 1, 2008.

10. Talbott, *Sell Now! The End of the Housing Bubble.*

11. Daniel Griswold, Stephen Slivinski, and Christopher Preble, "Six Reasons to Kill Farm Subsidies and Trade Barriers," The Cato Institute, February 1, 2006, http://www.freetrade.org/node/493.

12. Federal Election Commission, "Contributions from Selected Industries," The Center for Responsive Politics, March 20, 2008, http://www.opensecrets.org/pres08/select .asp?Ind=K02.

13. Obama Campaign, "Plan to Change Washington."

14. Ibid.

15. Ibid.

16. Ibid.

17. Ibid.

18. Obama for America, "Remarks of Senator Barack Obama at Cooper Union—Renewing the American Economy," March 27, 2008, http://www.barackobama .com/2008/03/ 27/remarks_of_senator_barack_obam_54.php.

CHAPTER FIVE—GLOBALIZATION AND JOBS

1. David Ricardo, *Principles of Political Economy and Taxation* (New York: Cosimo Classics, 2006).

2. Expat Focus, "India—Currency and Cost of Living," March 2008, http://www .expatfocus.com/expatriate-india-currency-costs.

3. Obama, *The Audacity of Hope*, 172–176.

4. Ibid., 172–176.

5. Obama Campaign, "Plan to Strengthen the Economy."

6. Obama Campaign, "Plan for Immigration."

7. Ibid.

8. Obama, *The Audacity of Hope*, 259–269.

CHAPTER SIX—GLOBAL WARMING AND ENERGY POLICY

1. Obama, *The Audacity of Hope*, 168.

2. Barack Obama, "Real Leadership for a Clean Energy Future," speech given in Portsmouth, New Hampshire, October 08, 2007, http://www.barackObama .com/2007/10/08/remarks_of_senator_barack_obam_28.php.

3. Obama Campaign, "Energy and the Environment," March 2008, http://www .barackobama.com/issues/energy/.

4. Ibid.

5. Ibid.

6. Ibid.

7. Obama, *The Audacity of Hope*, 165–168.

8. Ibid.

9. Obama Campaign, "Energy and the Environment."

10. Ibid.

11. Maya Jackson Randall and Andrea Thomas, "Paulson: 2008 to Be Difficult Year," *Wall Street Journal*, April 13, 2008, http://online.wsj.com/article/SB120800 39689631o415.html?mod=hps_us_whats_news.

12. Obama Campaign, "Energy and the Environment."

13. Ibid.

14. Obama for America, "Promoting A Healthy Environment," April 2008, http://www.barackobama.com/issues/pdf/EnvironmentFactSheet.pdf.

15. Obama Campaign, "Energy and the Environment."

16. Ibid.

17. Ibid.

18. Ibid.

19. Ibid.

20. Argyle Executive Forum, "Energy and Private Equity Forum," New York, 2007, http://www.execforum.net/events/eventimages/06.12.07/main.html.

21. Wikipedia. "List of Countries By Carbon Dioxide Emissions Per Capita," 2004, http://en.wikipedia.org/wiki/List_of_countries_by_carbon_dioxide_emissions_per _capita#List_of_countries_by_emissions.

22. Infoplease, "World Energy Consumption and Carbon Dioxide Emissions, 1990–2025," March 2008, http://www.infoplease.com/ipa/A0776146.html.

23. David Guggenheim, *An Inconvenient Truth*, 2006, Lawrence Bender Productions.

24. Michael Crichton, *State of Fear* (New York: Avon Books, 2005).

25. Obama for America, "Promoting A Healthy Environment."

26. Obama Campaign, "Energy and the Environment."

CHAPTER SEVEN—AFFORDABLE HEALTHCARE

1. Obama, *The Audacity of Hope*, 194.

2. Obama for America, "Barack Obama's Plan for a Healthy America," 2008, http://www.barackobama.com/issues/pdf/HealthCareFullPlan.pdf.

3. Obama Campaign, "Plan for a Healthy America," April 2008, http://www.barackobama.com/issues/healthcare/.

4. Obama for America, "Barack Obama's Plan for a Healthy America."

5. Long, Michael. August 11, 2004. *Hospitals Inundated With Uninsured as Emergency Room Visits Grow*. Healthy Living NYC. http://www.healthylivingnyc.com/article/21.

6. Obama Campaign, "Plan for a Healthy America."

7. Ibid.

8. Obama for America, "Barack Obama's Plan for a Healthy America."

9. Obama Campaign, "Plan for a Healthy America."

10. The National Coalition on Health Care, "Health Insurance Costs," 2008, http://www.nchc.org/facts/cost.shtml.

11. Obama, *The Audacity of Hope*, 183–186.

12. Obama, *Dreams From My Father*.

13. David M. Cutler, *Your Money or Your Life: Strong Medicine for America's Health Care System* (London: Oxford University Press, 2004).

14. See http://sentineleffect.wordpress.com/2007/12/01/health-mandates-a-talk-with-obama-health-advisor-david-cutler/.

15. Obama Campaign, "Plan for a Healthy America."

CHAPTER EIGHT—THE AGING OF THE POPULATION

1. Obama, *The Audacity of Hope*, 179.

2. Laurence J. Kotlikoff and Scott Burns, *The Coming Generational Storm: What You Need to Know about America's Economic Future* (Boston: MIT Press, 2005).

3. Obama, *The Audacity of Hope*, 179.

4. Peterson, *Running On Empty*, 33.

5. Obama Campaign, "Plan to Strengthen Retirement Security," Obama for America, http://www.barackobama.com/issues/socialsecurity/.

6. Michael Barone, "The Wealth of the Nation," *US News & World Report*, March 1, 2006, http://www.usnews.com/blogs/barone/2006/3/1/the-wealth-of-the-nation.html.

7. Karen C. Holden and Timothy M. Smeeding, "The Poor, the Rich, and the Insecure Elderly Caught in Between," *Milbank Quarterly*, vol. 68, no. 2, 1990, 191–219, http://www.ncbi.nlm.nih.gov/pubmed/2122199.

8. Barone, "The Wealth of the Nation."

9. Social Security Online, "Social Security Basics," Social Security Administration Press Office, March 28, 2008, http://www.ssa.gov/pressoffice/basicfact.htm.

10. Budget of the United States Government, Fiscal year 2008, Table S–7. Budget Summary by Category, Office of Management and Budget, http://www.whitehouse.gov/ omb/budget/fy2008/summarytables.html.

11. US Census Bureau, "United States Aging Demographics," UNC Institute on Aging, October 2006, http://www.aging.unc.edu/infocenter/slides/usaging.ppt#259,5,US Population Pyramids.

CHAPTER NINE—COOPERATION IS THE KEY

1. Obama, *The Audacity of Hope*, 55.

2. Ibid.

3. Ryan Lizza, "The Agitator—Barack Obama's Unlikely Political Education," *New Republic*, March 19, 2007, http://www.pickensdemocrats.org/info/TheAgitator_070319.htm.

4. Ibid.

5. Obama has not had a major policy speech on animal rights to my knowledge, but he did say he cared about animal rights very much in response to a question at a town hall meeting in Las Vegas on January 16, 2008.

6. Obama has come out against relaxing the rules on media concentration in metropolitan markets that would allow greater cross-ownership of media properties across television, radio and newspapers.

7. While he has not made a major policy statement about tobacco use, Obama himself quit smoking during his run for the presidency, for his children and as an example to Americans.

8. Wikipedia, "The Hunger Project," March 2008, http://en.wikipedia.org/wiki/The _Hunger_Project.

9. Transcript of Barack Obama's Speech at Nasdaq, *New York Times*, September 17, 2007, http://www.nytimes.com/2007/09/17/us/politics/16text-obama.html.

CHAPTER TEN—ETHICS AND ECONOMICS: MY BROTHER'S KEEPER

1. Keynote Address by Barack Obama, 2004 Democratic National Convention, July 26-29, 2004, http://www.americanrhetoric.com/speeches/convention2004/barack-obama2004dnc.htm.

2. Speech by Barack Obama, "Changing the Odds for Urban America," Washington, DC, July 18, 2007, http://www.barackobama.com/2007/07/18/remarks_of _senator _barack_obam_19.php.

3. Ibid.

4. Speech by Barack Obama, "A More Perfect Union," Constitution Center. Philadelphia, PA, March 18, 2008, http://www.barackobama.com/2008/03/ 18/remarks_of _senator_barack_obam_53.php.

5. John Steinbeck, *The Grapes of Wrath and Other Writings 1936-1941* (New York: Literary Classics, 1996), 655.

6. Lizza, "The Agitator – Barack Obama's Unlikely Political Education."

7. Obama, *The Audacity of Hope*, 325–352.

8. Ibid, 325.

9. Malcolm Gladwell, *The Tipping Point: How Little Things Can Make a Big Difference* (New York: Back Bay Books, 2002).

10. Speech by Barack Obama, "A More Perfect Union."

11. Speech by Barack Obama, "A Call to Serve," Mt. Vernon, Iowa, December 07, 2007, http://www.barackobama.com/2007/12/05/remarks_of_senator_barack_obam _36.php.

EPILOGUE

1. Obama, *The Audacity of Hope*, 361.

2. Duane R. Patterson, "Michelle Obama's Vision Of America," Townhall.com, February 15, 2008, http://hughhewitt.townhall.com/blog/g/a8b77fb9-4dd6-4045-9b43 -3c656cba2f38.

3. Jonathan Weisman, "Richardson Throws Support to Obama," *Washington Post*, March 22, 2008, http://www.washingtonpost.com/wp-dyn/content/story/2008/03/22/ST2008032200159.html?sid=ST2008032200159.

4. Speech by Barack Obama at the Dr. Martin Luther King Jr. National Memorial Groundbreaking Ceremony, November 13, 2006, http://usliberals.about.com/od/extraordinaryspeeches/a/ObamaMLK.htm.

ABOUT THE AUTHOR

JOHN R. TALBOTT is a former top investment banker for Goldman Sachs. For the last decade he has been writing full time as an author, publishing five books and numerous peer-reviewed academic journal articles on economics and politics. His first book, *Slave Wages* (1999) describes the threat that increased income and wealth inequality poses to America's ethical foundation. *The Coming Crash of the Housing Market* (McGraw Hill, 2003) was an amazon.com and *Business Week* bestseller that accurately predicted the current problems in the US housing and mortgage market. In *Where America Went Wrong And How to Regain Her Democratic Ideals* (Financial Times/Prentice Hall, 2004), John examines the importance of democratic institutions, both in the US and abroad, in promoting and maintaining a prosperous economy. *Sell Now! The End of the Housing Bubble* (St. Martin's Press, 2006) predicted the peak of home prices, placing the blame on unregulated lending institutions. *Obamanomics* (Seven Stories Press, 2008) shows how Barack Obama's policies will right the US economy, bring about housing, banking, and energy reform, and instigate social change.

John has served as an economic adviser to a number of developing countries, including Jordan and Russia. He has appeared live on CNN, Fox News, CNNfn, CNBC, MSNBC, and CBS, and has published articles in the *Wall Street Journal*, the *Boston Globe*, and the *Financial Times*. John graduated from Cornell University with a BS in Civil Engineering, worked for two years for Bechtel Corporation, and received his MBA from The Anderson School at UCLA, where he majored in finance. He can be reached at john-talbs@hotmail.com.

COMMENTS ABOUT JOHN R. TALBOTT AND HIS WORK

"Talbott is the author of two books that more or less foretold the pain homeowners are now experiencing. . . . So far, many of John Talbott's predictions have been spot-on."
—*Newsweek*, November 6, 2007

"When John Talbott's controversial book, *The Coming Crash in the Housing Market*, hit store shelves in 2003, the real estate industry—and everyone else who stood to profit from the dizzying rise in U.S. home prices—gave it a hostile reception . . . So, with subprime mortgage losses and credit woes now the No. 1 topic in the markets, what does the former Goldman Sachs investment banker see next for the housing market and the U.S. economy?"
—*Toronto Globe & Mail*, September 14, 2007

"*Sell Now! The End of the Housing Bubble* is a data-driven and analysis-rich thesis that convincingly debunks all the current theories that—at least on face value—provide a rationale for our recent boom in housing prices."
—Wharton Alumni Club, April 27, 2006

"Please read Talbott's book closely: Is your home at risk? Then quickly decide whether you can hang on in a housing collapse, a stock market bear and another long recession."
—Dow Jones Marketwatch, March 13, 2006

"Talbott blames (the overheated housing market on) lenders for throwing ever larger mortgages at home buyers while requiring ever smaller down payments. Indeed, Mr. Talbott seems to consider lending out of control, warning that consumers are up to their eyeballs in debt of all kinds. He fears that when the housing bubble bursts it could have huge effects on the economy. These post-bubble calamities are what really keep Mr. Talbott up at night, and his sobering book should inspire a little tossing and turning in the rest of us too."

—*Wall Street Journal*, June 4, 2003

ABOUT SEVEN STORIES PRESS

Seven Stories Press is an independent book publisher based in New York City, with distribution throughout the United States, Canada, England, and Australia. We publish works of the imagination by such writers as Nelson Algren, Russell Banks, Octavia E. Butler, Ani DiFranco, Assia Djebar, Ariel Dorfman, Annie Ernaux, Barry Gifford, Almudena Grandes, Elfriede Jelinek, Peter Plate, Lee Stringer, and Kurt Vonnegut, to name a few, together with political titles by voices of conscience, including the Boston Women's Health Book Collective, Noam Chomsky, Angela Davis, Stuart and Elizabeth Ewen, Coco Fusco, Martin Garbus, Human Rights Watch, Ralph Nader, Gary Null, Project Censored, Paul Robeson, Jr., Barbara Seaman, Gary Webb, and Howard Zinn, among many others. Our books appear in hardcover, paperback, pamphlet, and e-book formats, in English and in Spanish. We believe publishers have a special responsibility to defend free speech and human rights, and to celebrate the gifts of the human imagination, wherever we can.

For more information, visit our Web site at www.sevenstories.com, or write for a free catalogue to Seven Stories Press, 140 Watts Street, New York, NY 10013.